M000015264

If asked, most of us would say we want to be happy. Ask parents what they want for their children and the word 'happy' always comes up.

Being happy is actually quite another matter from wanting to be happy.

This fabulous book breaks down the various stages of happiness, making it much easier to understand the different levels and depths of happiness and how to attain them. It also shows how, paradoxically, the best way to be happy is not to seek it for oneself, which is an act of selfishness, but to bring happiness into the lives of others. Understanding how to do this and making a difference to the lives of our families, friends, children, co-workers and even strangers, is the purpose of this book.

I found it a joy to read and would recommend it to anyone searching for meaning in their life and it's a must for anyone involved with adults' and children's wellbeing.

—Claire Howell, Chief Executive and senior executive coach of REDCO Ltd

What I really like about *The Stairway to Happiness* is how fundamental ideas from philosophy have been made refreshingly accessible and married with modern cognitive psychology practices to provide helpful and valuable guidance on living a happier life while helping others to do the same.

The Stairway's five steps make intuitive sense and the examples from daily life enable the lessons to be put into practice more easily. I very much enjoyed reading this book.

—Mrs Lynn Paine, John G McLean Professor and Senior Associate Dean for International Development at Harvard Business School

The Stairway to Happiness is a fascinating, stimulating and inspiring piece of work. I read it all the way through until I finished it at 2 am!

The path of self-discovery within this book is a reminder of what is important, what really matters and what is worthy. It also provides an explanation of what happiness actually comprises and guidance on what to do about achieving it for oneself and for others.

This is a 'must read' for those with curiosity of mind and the courage to ask 'why?'

—Martin Hatcher, Former Executive Chairman,
Scansource Communications Ltd and MTV Telecoms

The Stairway to Happiness is a thoughtful and valuable guide for those of us who want to understand what constitutes happiness in life, how this can be accomplished and how to help others.

It is a sophisticated and wise book that combines insights from age-old Greek philosophy with contemporary scientific and psychological knowledge as well as practical advice with day-to-day examples. It also includes spiritual reflections to round off a very enjoyable read.

It is a very accessible book that I look forward to sharing and discussing with many of my personal and professional friends.

—Debbie Jaarsma, Professor Innovation and Research
in Medical Education, University Medical Centre,
Groningen, Netherlands

The Stairway to Happiness is a fascinating and novel combination of Philosophy, Psychology and Spirituality. It is where science meets spirituality.

Its strength is that it enables the reader to progress smoothly through these different approaches in a logical way and to learn how they are all connected and aligned with each other in a common message of hope and love.

While the final step, the Happiness of Harmony, is the most spiritual and arguably the most difficult as well as important, the reader is introduced gently and seamlessly into this more esoteric, yet vitally relevant world. She/he is left facing the key questions about who she really is, what her priorities should be and how she should address them. This is a revelation in Human Consciousness.

The Stairway to Happiness provides straightforward and valuable guidance on living a better, more peaceful, more harmonious and happier life. Its insights are refreshing.

As a Life Coach and Spiritual Teacher, I applaud this book and look forward to its extension and development into more and different media formats so as to spread the message as widely as possible and help people awaken to the true reality of existence. There is a real need for people to reconnect with the universe and with their soul and to learn to really live.

—Katey Lockwood, Life Coach and Spiritual
Teacher

Wise, insightful and packed with practical advice, *The Stairway to Happiness* has the potential to transform many lives for the better. It is unusual to find a book on a deep subject such as this which is easy to read and very accessible. I enjoyed reading it a lot and will keep it close at hand.

—Wei Huang, Independent investor and
strategist, Shanghai, China

This is a 'must-read' for anyone who has children and loved ones or, like many of us, has lived a life faced with challenges. Vernon shows us grace, acceptance, love and the stairway to a beautiful, fulfilling and happy life.

We will all continue to face challenges in our lives, but with The Stairway to Happiness as our guide, we will come out stronger and better on the other side.

—Joy Atkinson, President, Firmenich Body
Home Care North America, USA

The Stairway to Happiness resonates with my own experience in many respects. Combining classical wisdom, theory, theology and psychology with Vernon's own life experience results in an inspiring and yet practical book. I am grateful to have had the opportunity to share it and I have been able to consciously practice the steps almost immediately, not least with the stress of my three children's A level exams!

—The Revd Tina Molyneux, Associate Priest of the Church of England and mother of triplets

The Stairway to Happiness

Vernon Sankey

The
Stairway
to
Happiness

The five key steps on the Stairway to Happiness
and how to climb them

Vernon Sankey

Copyright © 2018 by Vernon Sankey

All rights reserved. No part of this publication may
be reproduced, stored in or introduced into a retrieval
system, or transmitted, in any form, or by any means
(mechanical, electronic, recording, photocopying or
otherwise) without the prior written permission of both
the copyright owner and publisher of this publication.
The uploading, scanning, and distribution of this
publication via the Internet or any other means without
the permission of the publisher is prohibited and
punishable by law.

ISBN: 978-1-9995972-0-7 (softcover)
ISBN: 978-1-9995972-1-4 (Kindle)
ISBN: 978-1-9995972-2-1 (EPUB)

Improve Your World Publishers Co Limited
www.improvemyworld.com

Front cover concept by Angela Godley

Book design by Jill Ronsley, Sun Editing & Book Design,
suneditwrite.com

Printed and bound in the United Kingdom

DEDICATION

The Stairway to Happiness is dedicated to those people who have a genuine passion for learning and growing, for helping and creating happiness for others and, in so doing, finding happiness for themselves. They will be people with a compassionate soul, who are kind and respectful, who appreciate what some call 'the little things' but which are what really matter most in life: a smile, a thank you, nature, simplicity, authenticity, friendship, peace, tolerance and love. They understand that we are all part of the same universe, their actions are guided by a sense of justice and truth and they are awake to what is truly 'real' and beautiful. I hope they will enjoy this book.

Begin at once to live life
and count each separate day
as a separate life.

—Seneca

CONTENTS

ACKNOWLEDGEMENTS

When I set out to write this book, encouraged by my family and friends, I had no idea how much enjoyment I would have and how much I would learn. Nor did I understand what was involved and how much help I would need! None of this could have been done without the kindness and enthusiasm of so many. They have taught me so much.

I am very grateful to my lovely wife and family for their constant support and love, their tolerance and their many valuable contributions. They epitomize so much of what the book is about.

I am also very grateful to my friends who, through their awareness, profound understanding and willingness to share have been instrumental in helping me write a book that is based on sound principles as well as set in a wider, more philosophical and spiritual context. They too are wonderful role-models.

All the anecdotes of the happiness of harmony are drawn from personal experiences involving family or friends and are truly heartfelt.

I would also like to thank my editor, Jill Ronsley, for her wonderful work and all her help and advice. It has been a great pleasure to work with someone so positive and professional.

The Stairway to Happiness

The
Stairway
to
Happiness

◇◇◇◇◇◇◇◇◇◇◇◇◇◇◇◇◇◇◇◇◇◇◇◇◇◇◇◇◇◇◇◇◇◇◇◇◇◇

Part 1

The purpose of life is happiness,
which is achieved by virtue, living according
to the dictates of reason, ethical and
philosophical training, self-reflection,
careful judgement and inner calm.

Very little is needed to make a happy life;
it is all within yourself, in your way of thinking.
Marcus Aurelius

A calm and humble life will bring
more happiness than striving for success
and the constant anxiety that comes with it.
Albert Einstein

The objective of *The Stairway to Happiness* is to consider the way human beings achieve differing levels and intensity of happiness, why they don't always succeed and what they can do to overcome obstacles and create a powerful and happy future for themselves and those around them.

The Stairway to Happiness is directed at all thinking human beings and is relevant to everyone. It has direct implications for children making their first steps in life as it has for adults of all ages, parents, students, people working in every profession, senior executives, leaders of our communities, the unemployed and the retired.

It is particularly appropriate for people who are wondering about their own mission in life, what they should do with their life, what future they really want and to what extent their life is a happy and fulfilled one or if they need some help and assistance.

At a time when we are frenetically rushing about trying to keep up and feeling that we are overwhelmingly lost, we seem to have little time to take stock. And yet it is precisely at such times that we need to do so.

The issues raised here are common to everyone and it is simply the manner and intensity with which they manifest themselves that differs. Just as the busy executive in the office needs to acquire the wisdom and skills to manage his life successfully and happily, so does the person at home—not just for themselves but more especially for others.

In Part 1, we explore the circumstances that create, nurture and promote happiness—the *five key steps*—as well as some of the potential dangers that lie in the way. Many of the situations described will be very familiar.

In Part 2, we explain how the mind works and some basic principles of cognitive psychology. We also describe and explain a number of techniques and methodologies that can be learnt and successfully deployed to overcome the problems as they occur at each stage of the journey.

As in all matters regarding successful outcomes, it is ultimately each person's own desire to learn and achieve change that dictates whether, and to what extent, they will succeed.

While *The Stairway to Happiness* will provide a guide and instructions, it is up to each person to decide to make the necessary effort. It is only through personal desire, effort and determination that change can happen.

If it's to be, it's up to me!

Why be happy?

Living a happy life does not mean that we have to be happy all the time, wandering about with a benign smile on our faces and living in an unreal utopia. Nor does it mean that we do not feel anger, irritation, sadness or any other human emotion.

Happiness is an emotion that, when allowed to develop and flourish, enables us to make the best of good times, for ourselves and for others. It also helps us to handle adversity, when it inevitably arises, more positively and with better results.

There are many other reasons why happiness is beneficial. Research has shown that happiness generates a wide range of important benefits to health, relationships, achievement, resilience, decision-making, creativity, responsibility and success.

Happiness also brings benefits to our environment. Research has also shown that happier people are more responsible in their behaviour, take less risky actions, are more attuned to the needs of others and their environment and are more likely to vote and do voluntary work.

Happiness is also contagious. Happy people lighten the atmosphere and help others around them become happier. A study in the *BMJ* (*British Medical*

Journal) found that the happiness engendered by happy people affects others across 'three degrees of separation', and thus has a positive effect on the mood of your friend's friend's friend.

Happiness attracts others and, as a result, attracts happier experiences. For that to happen, people need to understand the different levels and intensity of happiness that can exist and how to develop the attitude and skills to, simply, become happier. After all, people are unlikely to attract happiness if they are miserable, unsmiling, uncommunicative, testy or angry!

Happiness is about helping people live better lives and creating a society that is healthier, more creative, more generous, tolerant and harmonious. There has never been a greater need for this.

A very brief Greek historical perspective

Prior to Socrates, most ancient civilizations tended to have a rather pessimistic view of human existence and their own role on earth. They attributed success or failure to the happiness or anger of the gods, whichever ones they happened to believe in, and, over the centuries, there have been many.

Happiness was therefore a rare event dependent on the favour of the gods. It was not for mere mortals to seek to achieve happiness. This would have been seen as an act of excessive pride—hubris—to be met with retribution and disaster—nemesis.

So the gods, rather than the individual, were responsible for whatever happened—a wonderful way to abnegate responsibility for selfish actions. Note that we still use today the expression 'it's in the lap of the gods' when we feel there is nothing we can do.

However, the optimistic Socrates was the first known Western person to argue that happiness is attainable, and only attainable, by direct human effort. He advocated turning away from the pleasures of the body and concentrating on the nourishment of the soul by exercising conscious control over desires so as to be able to harmonize the other parts of the soul.

Developed carefully and conscientiously over time while living a moral rather than an immoral life, this method would pacify the mind and result in a divine-like state of tranquillity and inner happiness.

Socrates lived during a period of war and deprivation in an environment of cruelty, depravation and ignorance. This led him to question all aspects of his and his fellow citizens' existence and behaviour and raise evident social and ethical issues.

Socrates made himself very unpopular in Athens by challenging existing beliefs and preconceptions, most of which he felt were based on myth or rumour and were without logical foundation.

He would admit his ignorance and seek truth through a process of questioning. This was designed to expose ignorance and discover knowledge and wisdom—the basis of happiness.

His questions were straightforward but uncomfortable. Why do wealthy, high-born Greeks live a life of gluttony, cruelty and selfishness when fellow citizens are dying of disease and hunger? Why is it so important to be moral when we see all around us immoral people who seem to be benefitting more? What, exactly, is happiness? Is happiness to be sought for itself as a virtue or is it the result of achieving 'success'? Or is it something else altogether? What really happens to the soul after death? Does anyone really know?

All these questions are, of course, still equally relevant today.

The price he paid for his open quest for truth was to be sentenced to death for 'corrupting youth'. True to his beliefs, he did not blame the gods for his fate but went cheerfully to his death, which was by his own hand, knowing he had kept faith with his beliefs.

He considered that death represented the ultimate release of the soul from the limitations of the body and continued discussing philosophical concepts with his friends right up to the end.

Plato, Socrates' pupil and the person from whom we learn most about Socrates, believed, like his teacher, that human beings must be consciously moral to be truly happy. Immoral people cannot achieve happiness.

For Plato, being moral meant developing the four cardinal virtues of wisdom, courage, moderation and justice. The wise (not didactic), courageous (not reckless), self-controlled (not manic) and just (not uncompassionate) person is thus at peace, fulfilled and ultimately happy.

Without justice there can be no peace.

Given a choice, we all prefer to have a healthy rather than unhealthy body—a perfectly rational point of view. Similarly, our soul needs to be healthy and requires harmony and justice to be healthy.

The just soul acquires a psychological harmony that maintains balance whatever the circumstances.

Plato distinguished different types or steps of happiness and redefined happiness in terms of internal rather than external characteristics.

For Plato's pupil Aristotle, happiness is not an abstract idea but based on personal experience and practical actions, whose ultimate achievement is the discovery of happiness.

Happiness is the meaning and purpose of life, the whole aim of human existence.

Although seemingly self-contradictory, true happiness is not achieved by seeking it for itself. Rather it is the by-product of and depends on an active life filled with positive, moral and just decisions.

These decisions are taken in the full realization that the individual and the individual alone is responsible for the outcome of each decision and must live with its consequences.

As these decisions become wiser, more responsible and beneficial, so too the individual discovers new truths, expands his or her consciousness and moves closer to a happier mental state and the happiness of self-actualization.

Socrates, Plato and Aristotle's thinking also gave rise to another major philosophical movement, Stoicism, which will feature significantly in Part 2.

Stoicism was founded by Zeno of Citium in Athens in the early 3rd century BC. It was developed by Epictetus, Seneca and the Roman Emperor Marcus

Aurelius, the last of the so-called Five Good Emperors, and taken up with enthusiasm during the Roman Empire and by the early Christians before declining with the development of the Christian Church's own teachings.

Stoicism re-emerges during the Renaissance and again in the modern era. Current cognitive behavioural methodologies and practices have close and direct links to those of Stoicism.

Stoicism is a philosophy of personal ethics and a way of life, informed by logic and subject to the laws of nature. This means conducting a virtuous life guided by logic, wisdom, self-control and clear judgment in the face of adversity, in harmony with the divine order of the universe and respecting nature and all people.

According to Stoic teachings, the path to happiness is to be found in accepting each moment as it occurs, understanding that the only two things we can ever control are our thoughts and our actions and that these should be governed by our self-control, resilience, empathy for fellow human beings and the four cardinal virtues, as espoused by Plato, of Wisdom, Courage, Justice and Temperance.

According to the Stoics, everyone and everything is a manifestation of the same universe; so human beings should live in peace and harmony with each other, because all men alike are products of nature. Improving a person's ethical and moral behaviour is central to Stoic philosophy, including the control of anger, envy, jealousy and all those sentiments which detract from a happy life.

Your life depends on the quality of your thoughts.
Marcus Aurelius

Since the only things we can truly control are our own thoughts and actions, it is by understanding how our mind works and training our thoughts to make judgments in accordance with sound and deeply held *values* that we can live a happier life.

A happy life **lets go** *what we cannot control (and which tends to make us stressed and unhappy), focuses on the present and what we* **can** *actually achieve, appreciates* **what we have** *rather than yearning for what we cannot have and rejoices in the beauty of life.*

Seneca mirrors these thoughts when he writes: **'True happiness is to enjoy the present ... without anxious dependence upon the future.'** And again: **'It is not the man who has too little, but the man who craves more, that is poor.'**

However, despite this overview of Greek philosophy, *The Stairway to Happiness* is not intended to be a learned treatise on ethics, rather it seeks to explore the levels of intensity and depth of the different types of happiness that human beings can experience against the background of and with the benefit of the wisdom passed down through the ages.

Throughout the *five key steps*, we see that the thoughts of Socrates, Plato and Aristotle, Epictetus, Seneca and Marcus Aurelius are as relevant today as they have ever been and provide wisdom and direction on what human beings need to master. Human nature has not changed in the intervening years.

The teachings of these philosophers remain totally appropriate, although they lived nearly 2,500 years ago. They could be called the first cognitive psychologists in that they sought to understand how the mind works and what processes needed to be learnt to achieve understanding, success and ultimately happiness. Socrates said: **'An unexamined life is not worth living.'** The *five key steps* examines an important aspect of life, the search for happiness.

As part of that search, *The Stairway to Happiness* offers practical advice, guidance and some techniques that will help individuals determine their own pathway to happiness. In so doing it explores the risks, difficulties and obstacles that will present themselves along the way and provides practical guidance and skills on how to deal with them.

> *I cannot teach anybody anything;*
> *I can only make them think.*

It is for the reader to think for themselves and decide their own course of action.

UNDERSTANDING
THE STEPS

THE FIRST STEP:

INSTANT GRATIFICATION

When baby is born, she cries. She needs comfort and food. Whenever she cries, she needs something. Once satiated—the very first step of happiness—she (normally!) calms down and goes to sleep. Until, that is, she needs the next thing. As she grows she begins to respond by smiling and, gradually, the needs turn to wants. And crying brings results: the first incidence of instant gratification, the first step of the stairway of happiness.

As the baby becomes a toddler, child, adolescent, youth, she learns quickly that she can experience some level of happiness by wanting and getting.

But this happiness is rather short-lived and requires constant topping up. It is also rather shallow in its intensity, without substance or depth.

The same happens with adults. In a world where it is easier and easier to acquire material objects and borrow money to do so, the happiness of possession or instant gratification is all too easy to achieve. It requires little energy or effort. Just a few clicks.

I want. I get. How wonderful!

Only it isn't that wonderful. Yes, it's terrific to have that new toy for a short while. But, like a drug, the effects soon wear off. We get bored with the toy. It goes to the back of the cupboard with all the other discarded items and we forget all about it. Our homes are full of such items. They end up in the charity shop, handed down or on the tip.

The happiness we experience is very transient. Is it all that awful? No, not really, even if it is rather wasteful. So what's the problem?

There are two real problems: one is that it is too easy to believe the happiness that ensues, however slight, has value; and the other is where it can lead to, if unchecked.

Caught in the spiral of wanting and getting, just like a drug, the opposite of happiness then occurs: we become unhappy if we don't get, feel miserable and look around to see who we can blame for our predicament.

Resentment, anger, envy all have space to play their role with significant negative implications for ourselves and our environment.

If our child isn't helped to understand that getting whatever she wants whenever she wants is wrong, we have the makings of the classic spoilt, dysfunction-al child. Children need to be helped to learn this as soon as possible.

Instant gratification can have serious downsides. It can lead to addictive cravings, indebtedness, family and marital discord, disharmony.

Addictive cravings come in many forms but all are the result of the desire for ever-increasing instant gratification that is out of control. Behaviour then becomes compulsive and habitual, the need seem-ingly insatiable. When added to the pressures of social media, which accentuate the issues, the overwhelming sense of unhappiness can become overwhelming.

In the case of vanity, the need always to appear better, more fashionable, fitter, thinner, and so on brings many risks—from spending excessive sums of money on personal appearance, clothes, diets or surgi-cal interventions to very serious mental problems that require hospitalization.

It is very concerning to know that unprecedented numbers of young people suffer from depression and other stress-related anxieties.

What starts off as a perfectly reasonable need to appear smart, healthy, modern and attractive becomes an obsession that takes greater and greater priority, of-ten requiring more and more money to finance, thus causing imbalance, disharmony and unhappiness to the person and those around them.

This brings us to the question of money. Money is itself neutral. It acquires value only in what it can do or be used for. Acquiring it, or any other possession, just for its own sake is not a path that leads to happiness. How many things do we actually need?

Although its absence can clearly lead to unhappiness, money in and of itself has no value.

It can, however, be used to achieve worthwhile objectives.

Socrates said that a wise person will use money in the right way in order to make life better, while an ignorant person will be wasteful and use money poorly, ending up worse than before. Money is only good when used wisely, for a purpose that is beneficial. This is part of leading a moral, balanced existence.

Instant gratification, therefore, is a very early stage of happiness with limited value and many downsides. We do derive an element of pleasure from treats, and there is nothing wrong with that. But there needs to be a proper balance to avoid creating the spoilt child syndrome or the stressed-out adult.

Human beings need to learn the risks of instant gratification and how to deal with them positively.

THE SECOND STEP:

THE HAPPINESS OF ACHIEVING

While the first level of happiness is limited in scope, energy and effect, the second step—the happiness of achieving—has more depth. It requires more effort and its effects are longer lasting. It is also a building block of essential personal development and growth, requiring more energy, application and drive.

Let's go back to our child. She goes to school and begins to learn. She learns to talk, play, sing, dance, and each time she learns something new, she achieves and experiences a sense of happiness, a happiness made greater by the congratulations she receives. She feels good about herself and wants to achieve more frequently.

Successful children exude happiness and this has contagious effects on others, who are drawn and attracted to them. This can also incite jealousy from others, often those less able than themselves, so they need to learn new skills to deal with this. These new skills are closely associated with steps three and four.

All being well, however, the achievements will continue throughout her life as she succeeds—in concerts, plays, sports and exams and receives awards, diplomas, medals, appointments and promotions.

Each achievement will allow her to feel a deeper, longer-lasting level of happiness, which has more value than before. It requires more of our higher efforts to achieve. It requires more intense levels of energy and the ability to set and achieve goals with the attendant skills of imagination and visualization.

Who cannot remember a time when they achieved something special, something that required real effort and the pride they felt when they achieved it? It is easy for memories of such events to be recalled many years later with great clarity and a revived sense of pride and satisfaction. This was also the stimulus for more effort and more achievement, leading to more successes.

At this stage, we should ask the question, What is success? Is success achieving our goals? Is success achieving happiness? Does that mean the greater the success, the greater the level of happiness? Can we in fact be truly happy?

While the second step—the happiness of achieving—is a major move forward and provides a significantly enhanced experience of happiness, it is not sufficient in itself to provide life-long happiness or the harmony of the soul that Socrates describes.

The quest for success and its attendant recognition is finite.

Take the successful sportsperson, famous actor or artist, the brilliant politician or the successful business executive, they can only rest on their laurels for so long. The adulation they enjoyed may not last. They are only as good as their last achievement and the disappointment of not being able to continue at such a high level can be devastating. They cannot expect to be happy ever after. On the contrary, as with instant gratification but after a somewhat longer period of time, the happiness of achievement turns to the unhappiness of the 'has-been'.

Unless they learn to step up to the third and fourth levels they will not avoid the emptiness of diminishing past achievements with the dissatisfaction that this brings. There is no such thing as a happy retirement if there is no further activity or purpose: only regret, disappointment, even depression.

Socrates believed that happiness could only be achieved by human effort that is rooted in deep reflection. If we want to find greater happiness, we need to understand deeply where we want to go at whatever stage of life we are. We need to determine what efforts we want and need to make—with our energies, our talents, our lives—to achieve a meaningful future. For this to happen we need to set and reset our goals.

THE THIRD STEP:

THE HAPPINESS OF GIVING

Acquiring and achieving, the two first steps on the stairway to happiness, are essentially inner directed. They are primordially selfish. They are about wanting and achieving for oneself.

Achieving is about effort and diligence, determination and personal sacrifice—all admirable and necessary virtues and vital for the progress of humankind. It could be argued that these virtues are indeed humanity's very foundation and the essence of progress. All very worthy. There's nothing wrong with that. But there is a major risk.

Being essentially focused on the self rather than on others creates an ever-increasing risk of our life getting out of proportion. This manifests itself in wanting to achieve purely for the personal acclaim and fame it provides or for the sheer accumulation of things, as if a heap of objects is a reflection of an individual's greatness. Achievement risks becoming an exercise in vanity.

Achieving at all costs, winning no matter what or achieving results in whatever way are traps for the unwise and unwary. This is especially so when 'achieving' becomes 'achieving more than others'.

At this point, achieving for its own sake becomes manic, stressful and negative, creating unhappiness for the individual and, more particularly, for those around him or her, for whom life can become intolerable.

There is disharmony of the soul leading to serious health risks, dysfunction and misalignment, burn-out, family and marital problems and unhappiness.

To avoid this and return the soul to a harmonious state, we arrive at the third step, the happiness of giving.

This third step is the first one that focuses on others and their happiness, not our own. This is the first step that sees altruism as a virtue. It is next on the stairway and it is *the* critical step forward.

Paradoxically, through the happiness we can bring to others, this is also where we create a higher level of happiness for ourselves.

The happiness of others becomes the focus of our energy. Our own happiness becomes a by-product, but a by-product that has more depth than anything that has gone before.

Having acquired and achieved in the first two steps, the happiness of giving, or giving back, is vital for moving forward. It is also deeper, stronger and much longer lasting.

Giving becomes more rewarding than receiving—the exact opposite of step one. Not only is the happiness engendered by this more perennial but, once understood and appreciated, it provides a platform for ever-lasting benefit.

Age is not the issue here, but it has everything to do with maturity. Who has not seen children, even small children, help others with small tasks or share their toys? Or even ask an adult, in genuine interest, how they are and how their day has been, while smiling at them and making them feel good?

Such acts are all acts of giving, where the focus is not on oneself but on another. The so-called small gestures, such as smiling, saying hello, saying please and thank you, giving a seat to an older or infirm person, are as much acts of giving as voluntary work, caring for people or the environment, helping others with their problems, enjoying others' successes, contributing to charities, setting up foundations for worthy causes, and so on.

If you want to feel happy, do something nice for somebody—it will have its own rewards.

This is also the first step where human warmth and empathy are manifested directly, qualities that bring support, cheer and, yes, happiness to others.

All these acts of giving imply giving of oneself. They are the active, conscious, responsible decisions that bring in their wake a level of fulfilment and happiness that is intense and heightened.

This is what Aristotle means when he says happiness depends on an active life filled with positive, morally responsible actions.

There is no room for passivity here. This is about making and taking positive decisions and living with the consequences. It requires great energy and a different way of life.

This is where the most difficult questions start to be asked: 'Who am I?' 'What do I want to be?' 'Why?' 'What are my goals?' 'How do I want to conduct my life?' 'What sort of human being do I want to be?' 'What do I want to leave behind?' These are all questions that test us profoundly and are uncomfortable. They also need to be answered.

For happiness to exist to its full intensity, the answer has to come from deep personal reflection and a conscious list of priorities and goals that, for the third step, require to be both inner and outer directed. How do I want to live my life and what impact can it or will it have on others? How can that impact be beneficial and contribute to the happiness of others?

Having reflected on our choices, we have to be able to confirm that we have made them 'because this is what I choose to do after proper reflection'. In other words, 'This is my choice,' 'This is who I am and want to be,' 'These are my decisions,' 'This is my own commitment and no one else's.'

Yes, there will be sacrifices, but these sacrifices are willingly and happily accepted since they are the outcome of our serious intent.

Without doing this, we merely drift. Life tomorrow will be much like life today. Nothing much happens and nothing much changes.

At some stage in the future, however, we may suddenly wake up and realize that life has passed us by. If everything we encounter in our daily lives is familiar and unchallenging, then our lives carry on automatically and the days seem to fly past, almost at an accelerated pace.

Then, at some stage, we'll say: 'Whatever happened to my life?' 'Where did it all go?' 'What could I have done differently?' 'What a waste!'

Understanding why this happens, how to manage this process and the techniques to apply to live a purposeful and happier life, lie at the core of Part 2 of *The Stairway to Happiness*.

THE FOURTH STEP:

THE HAPPINESS OF RELATIONSHIPS

The fourth step has many layers and, like an escalator, traverses all five steps. This is the happiness that comes from relationships.

By relationships we mean any and all occasions where we interact with others, whether one-on-one or in groups. This includes partners, friends, siblings, family, clubs, associations, teams, companies and all those instances where, by coming together in a relaxed, mutually supportive, open and transparent environment, groups of human beings can create the conditions where each experiences a high level of happiness.

Happiness, in these circumstances, is determined by the quality of the relationships and, most importantly, the trust that exists between individuals. If the level of trust is low, the relationship will inevitably suffer and the opportunity for happiness will evaporate. If, on the other hand, the level of trust is high, the chance of fulfilment becomes that much greater.

We need to understand how to build and nurture trust and create an environment where trust flourishes.

Take our child. Her happiness is dependent on her relationship with, trust in and love of her mother, father, parent or guardian and the alignment and harmony that her parents display.

As she grows, her happiness becomes also dependent on her relationship with siblings, friends, classmates, student friends, boy- or girlfriends, partners and work and team colleagues.

As she learns that this unity and alignment matters, so too she needs to learn how to manage the relationships that lead to harmony. If our child grows up in an environment where trust is absent, she risks growing up frightened, timid, inward looking, pessimistic, unhappy. Her confidence will suffer as will her future happiness.

The key then lies in her growing in a trusting, optimistic environment where she can grow healthily and develop autonomy and initiative as she begins to understand the importance of interpersonal relationships.

As she develops her own identity, she learns how to create relationships with people of very different backgrounds, with different viewpoints, energies and dreams in a positive environment.

She will learn how to say no or disagree in a way that does not cause offence. She will learn how to handle difficult people and situations and make friends easily.

The Harvard Study of Adult Development, perhaps the longest study of adult life ever undertaken, came up with the clearest message: good relationships keep us healthier and happier. Social connections are vital to life and wellbeing, while loneliness kills.

People who have close, warm relationships with their partner, friends, communities and colleagues are happier, healthier and live on average longer than their colleagues who are less well connected and have less well developed relationships.

Although loneliness is often associated with old age, it is not the reserve of older people—far from it. People can be lonely in a crowd or in a marriage. High conflict marriages are toxic for health and often even worse than divorce.

It is not the number of friends that a person has, or whether they are, or are not, in a committed relationship that matters, but the quality, warmth and affection of those relationship. The better the relationship, the more protective to health. A similar conclusion was found in a study by the University of Virginia published in the journal *Child Development* on young people from the ages of fifteen to twenty-five.

Both studies found that not only did good, trusting relationships help protect the body, they also helped protect the mind.

Good relationships are not peaceful all the time. On the contrary, the ability to disagree and argue fervently is fundamental to mutual consideration. Trust, affection and dependability, however, are the keys to good relationships and overcome all arguments.

There isn't time—so brief is life—for bickerings,
apologies, heartburnings, callings to account.
There is only time for loving—
and but an instant, so to speak, for that.
Mark Twain

A word about **Love**: Deep relationships are the substance of love and a source of great happiness. The love that partners feel for each other is a source of real happiness, as is the love of parents and grandparents for children and grandchildren or friends for each other.

In many respects, this happiness is also close to the third stage of happiness, the happiness of giving, in that true love involves giving of oneself and forgiving, trusting and being trusted, caring and being cared for, guiding and helping others and being guided and helped in return.

Love mirrors the five steps. It can be purely about instant gratification. It can be about success. Or it can be about giving and receiving—enhanced by deep caring and accompanied by a sense of peace, harmony and joy.

Love leads to and is also a fundamental part of the fifth stage, the happiness of harmony, beauty and serenity, the love of our world, an understanding that we are all part of a much greater universal truth.

The English language is rich in words to describe complicated emotions and objects with great precision: except for 'love', for which there is only one word.

The Ancient Greeks, on the other hand, had several words for love and would not have understood how we can use the same word to mouth 'I love you' in a romantic setting while casually signing an email 'lots of love'!

In many respects the different Greek words for love relate directly to the different stages of happiness.

The first kind of love is *eros*, representing sexual passion and desire. *Eros* provides instant, intense, short-term happiness. But the Greeks considered *eros* potentially hazardous and irrational, leading to disharmony through loss of control, obsession and ultimately pain and suffering. *Eros* is the instant gratification of love, providing immediate happiness that dissipates rapidly and with attendant risks, if it is not accompanied by deeper loving emotions.

The second type of love is *philia* or deep friendship. This love is the bond found between friends, brothers- and sisters-in-arms, team colleagues and siblings. It is characterized by strong relationships, profound trust and fierce loyalty where friends are prepared to make sacrifices for each other, are willing to share emotions, pain and happiness.

The third type, which is along similar lines to *philia*, is *storge*, which is the deep love felt by parents and their children, characterized by similar relationships of trust, devotion, sacrifice and sharing.

The fourth variety is *pragma*, the mature love reflecting the deep understanding that develops between partners who have been together for a long time and who have shared many experiences and adventures together.

They understand each other completely and know when to compromise, be patient, forgiving and tolerant as a result of the deep love that has grown between them.

Pragma is about giving love rather than just receiving it. It is about making the effort to nurture, maintain and strengthen the loving relationship that deepens and develops over time.

Three of these types of love—*philia, storge* and *pragma*—are encompassed in the happiness of relationships, the fourth step on *the Stairway*.

The fifth type of love is *philautia*, or self-love. This love has two very different aspects.

One aspect, closer to instant-gratification, is related to narcissism, where the individual loves themselves, becomes self-obsessed, vain and more focused on personal aggrandizement, fame and recognition.

The other, which is part of the fourth step and closer to self-actualization (see next step), is related to the idea that if the individual is secure in themselves, comfortable about who they are and thus happy about themselves, they will be better able to give love to others.

*All friendly feelings for others are
an extension of a man's feelings for himself.*
Aristotle

If you do not love (that is, know who you are and have confidence in) yourself, it is difficult to feel love for anyone else.

Buddhist philosophy refers to this as 'self-compassion'.

Searching all directions with one's awareness, one finds no one dearer than oneself.
In the same way, others are dear to themselves.
So one should not hurt others if one loves oneself.
Buddha

The sixth variety of love is *agape* or selfless, universal love—the closest to the fifth step, the happiness of harmony. This love is extended to all people, irrespective of who they are. It recognizes that we are all part of one universe.

CS Lewis called it 'gift love', the highest form of Christian love. In Theravada Buddhism it is 'universal loving kindness'. This is about empathy for mankind and care for all, family and strangers alike. *Agape* was translated into Latin as *caritas* from which we have the word charity.

Faith, hope and charity,
but the greatest of these is charity.
St Paul

This fourth step, the happiness of relationships and love, permeates all the other steps and is fundamental to enabling progress to be made from step to step.

It provides our existence and world with colour, hope, security and warmth. Even though we may be achieving a high level of happiness through giving, this is considerably enhanced if we supplement it with the happiness of relationships.

The intensity of happiness rises exponentially as we climb the steps and the earlier steps appear very limited by comparison.

THE FIFTH STEP:

THE HAPPINESS OF HARMONY

As we have moved up the steps of happiness and reached a very high level at the fourth step, we may feel that this is as far as we want to go, and there is no need to climb any further.

Indeed, achieving the fourth step provides an intensity of happiness of great depth.

There is, though, a fifth step—the happiness of harmony—a step that leads still further than the previous four.

With the fifth step, and in parallel with the development of our relationships and our experience of the love associated with them, we become increasingly aware that we are part of a much, much greater universe, where there is infinite beauty.

In this universe there is beauty everywhere: in people, art, writing, music, sculpture, dance, colours and textures, fragrances, food, plants and animals, the skies at night, rivers and waterfalls, the planets and the infinite twinkling of stars, even in silence.

There is beauty all around, if we only take the trouble to see and look, hear and listen, touch and feel.

This is not intended to be a romantic or new age description of an impossible utopia. The happiness of harmony brings together all the previous steps and adds to it a greater, universal context. It is about taking pleasure in admiring and enjoying what is already everywhere and all around us, and which we have forgotten or never had time to really see, hear, touch or experience. It is taking pleasure in the so-called simple things of life.

In a world where we lead hurried and harried lives and are bombarded by a continuous stream of negative stories, it is understandable that we have little time to grasp that there are different levels of happiness, let alone to set aside or find time for happiness at all.

Stop for a minute.

The fifth step is a recognition that we are part of something much greater than that which we generally experience and which, if we take time to understand and explore in combination with the previous steps, leads us to still higher levels of happiness.

To experience this, we need to develop enhanced skills of being—that is being able, when we choose to, to live in the moment, not worrying about tomorrow or yesterday; to accept ambiguity and that we don't have the answer to everything (or to anything according to Socrates). It means to experience, quietly and serenely, life all around us—from the simplicity of the flowers in the fields to the magnificence of humanity's greatest triumphs; to learn to use all our senses so as to appreciate to the full all that the world has to offer; to recognize that we are really very tiny in the context of our extraordinary universe; and to be humble and grateful for what we have.

> *Dwell on the beauty of life, watch the stars*
> *and see yourself running with them.*

If we can combine the relationships and love of the fourth step with the beauty, sanctity and harmony of the fifth, we will be close to achieving the self-actualization that is the goal of this step.

Self-actualization does not have to be about a guru-like transcendental status or to involve any mystical sensory powers.

The term 'self-actualization' was coined by A. Maslow in his book, Motivation and Personality, in which he describes the characteristics of the self-actu-alized person. They are people who

1. are comfortable with and embrace the un-known and the ambiguous;

2. accept themselves for who they are and know their own flaws;

3. set priorities and goals and enjoy the jour-ney, not just the destination;

4. are unconventional but without seeking to disturb, hurt or shock;

5. are motivated by personal and communal growth, not by the satisfaction of needs;

6. have a wider purpose; an unselfish mission concerned with the good of mankind;

7. work within a framework of values that are broad and are not concerned by trivialities;

8. are grateful for what they have and maintain a fresh sense of wonder towards the universe;

9. have deep, profound interpersonal relations regardless of class, education, race, colour, political or religious belief;

10. are humble and keen to learn from people who can teach them something;

11. are responsible for themselves and make up their own minds based on their own code of ethics;

12. are not perfect!

Perfect human beings simply do not exist; and it would be a very colourless world if they did.

Many of the characteristics of self-actualized people are those evoked in the previous steps; for example, they set goals and priorities, develop strong relationships and are responsible adults.

In the fifth step, self-actualization is about enjoying the journey and learning to enjoy and find real happiness in the simple but wondrous occasions provided by the universe.

There is great happiness to be experienced in the world: in a walk with a partner, friend or family along the beach; listening to the waves breaking on the shore; smelling and tasting the fresh, ozone-rich air while admiring the clouds on the horizon; enjoying a picnic with family or friends on a hillside in the country, enjoying the view of the river and hills beyond.

There is great joy in listening to the happy sounds of children and feeling the warmth of the grass as the heady, fragrance of lavender wafts all around; being at a lively dinner with friends in a relaxed atmosphere, where there is a shared sense of fun and warmth; lying on the ground in the late evening, looking at the twinkling stars and constellations in the infinite expanse of space;

There is a wonderful sense of peace just walking in the park or reading a good book under the trees; embracing and cuddling a loved one; joining a family reunion where all the members share in a magical sense of warmth, togetherness and love; and being involved with almost anything that has beauty, calm, serenity and love.

> **Là, tout n'est qu'ordre et beauté,**
> **luxe, calme et volupté.**
> **—'L'invitation au voyage' from**
> ***Les Fleurs du Mal,* Charles Baudelaire**

By using their power of imagination and visualization, everyone has the capacity to learn how to find and experience peace, tranquillity and happiness in simple, free, yet often overlooked situations and circumstances. Everyone can learn, like Socrates and the Stoics, to transpose themselves into what is, in effect, another world, an inner world they can inhabit whenever they wish and whenever they feel the need to escape from the so-called real external world, in order to find harmony, peace, happiness and their own paradise—either by themselves or with other like-minded souls. It's not a place so much as a state of mind or wonder.

I have deliberately not raised specific theological or theosophical matters, even though they are, of course, entirely pertinent to this subject. The reason is that whatever our religious beliefs, we are all seeking happiness. *The Stairway to Happiness* is intended to be complementary to and not in conflict with any peace-loving religion, nor is it intended to offend anyone. It does not suggest that any particular theology is more or less appropriate. That is up to individuals to decide.

However hard it is to believe at times, all religions seek to find true happiness in one form or another. Most religions have their version of 'heaven', the ultimate place of peace—whether it is *Brahman, moksha,* nirvana or paradise, the 'celestial kingdom' or the New Jerusalem.

Earth has no sorrow that heaven cannot heal.
Thomas Moore

The Stairway *to* Happiness

◇◇◇

PART 2

Socrates said: 'The unexamined life is not worth living.'

In Part 1, we examined:

1. what happiness is

2. why it is so important

3. how Socrates and his successors viewed happiness

4. what the five different and ascending steps are

5. what each step can provide in terms of intensity, duration and quality as we climb the stairway.

We also explored the benefits and some of the many pitfalls that can occur on the way up the steps and learnt the importance of effort and achievement, giving back, relationships and enjoying all the things that we have rather than those we do not have but mistakenly yearn for and then stress over.

We need to learn to desire what we already have; then we will have all we need.

*Love that only which happens to thee
and is spun with the thread of thy destiny.
For what is more suitable?*
Marcus Aurelius

In Part 2, we will see what understanding, skills, techniques and methods we need to acquire and develop in order to gain the most from each step and unblock obstacles as we move up.

We need to learn these lessons for our own health, wellbeing and inner harmony so as to be better able to manage, appreciate and enjoy our lives through all its vicissitudes—the ups as well as the inevitable downs.

Perhaps more especially, we need to learn these lessons for the sake of those around us whose happiness is also our responsibility. This is also our opportunity to do good things, to teach others what we learn, to make, appreciate and enhance our environment and to make others happier.

The subject of happiness is by no means a new subject and libraries are filled with self-help books, magazines and pamphlets with a vast range of recipes, suggestions, systems and recommendations. Many are indeed excellent, based on sound principles and contribute to understanding. I have found, however, that it is not always easy to relate the advice provided to specific issues and the bewildering array of suggestions are at times either too complicated or too simplistic to enable the reader to make real progress or understand **why** they might or might not be progressing, **what** the issues really are that they should be tackling and **how** to go about addressing them.

Part 2 of The Stairway to Happiness seeks to provide practical advice to enable the reader to:

1. understand **why** certain patterns of behaviour occur and re-occur, in other words to understand what is happening in the mind and how the mind functions

2. learn what to **do** to address these patterns of behaviour and change them if required.

The guidance provided in Part 2 is based on personal learning and experience and on methods that have been tried and tested over many years in a variety of circumstances and with a variety of customers—from comprehensive corporate change programs to one-on-one coaching.

Hopefully you will find that a dose of common sense has also been liberally sprinkled!

Some of the guidance is directly related to specific issues in individual steps and some is 'transversal', in the sense that the processes and skills are relevant across all the steps.

THE FIRST STEP:

INSTANT GRATIFICATION AND AN INTRODUCTION TO SOME BASIC CONCEPTS OF COGNITIVE PSYCHOLOGY

Before we look into each step, we need some basic background understanding of what happens in the mind, why and how.

Let us take our baby again. She cries whenever she needs food, comfort or changing and mother or father obliges. As she develops, she learns very quickly, subconsciously, that crying produces results.

This is the first manifestation of instant gratification. Although this is subconscious it is still very relevant and is necessary, natural, instinctive and beneficial to baby's survival, growth and development.

But baby also needs to learn, fairly quickly, that Mum or Dad are not 'on tap' every minute of the day and night (at least after the initial few days!). This is good neither for her nor her parents and if this pattern of behaviour and expectation persists, problems will soon ensue. Why?

> *Here comes the first opportunity*
> *to learn something important*
> *that goes across all the steps.*

> *Our subconscious mind controls*
> *almost everything that we do.*

Our subconscious mind is the automatic internal controller of our lives. It is permanently on duty and, based on the knowledge it has acquired and is constantly acquiring from us, directs our actions and activities without our having to even think about them.

That is why we do not have to think to get out of bed, switch the alarm off, get washed, brush teeth, get dressed, drink our coffee, go to work, say hello, smile, attend meetings, go home, put out the rubbish, switch on the TV or look at our messages. We do it all automatically.

You only have to look at the faces of fellow commuters to realize that most are on autopilot and will probably have little or no recollection of the journey after it is completed.

Sometimes we try to override our subconscious mind but fail to do so. How many times, for example, have we consciously decided *not* to do or say something—'I won't raise that subject,' 'I won't send that text,' 'I shouldn't talk about x,'—only, a few minutes later, to say or do that very thing?

That is because our subconscious mind, which is a fast and powerful learner and designed to help us and keep us 'normal', is leading us in the way it believes we want to go based on our previous actions and pattern of behaviour—otherwise known as our habits, attitudes, beliefs and expectations.

Moreover, our subconscious mind cannot process a negative, so trying *not* to do something will not be helped by our subconscious mind—quite the opposite—with the result that the thought remains in our mind and we act on it a little later, when our conscious mind has moved on to something else.

(Everyone knows if you ask someone *not* to think of a pink elephant, this is precisely the thought that will be come into in their mind as the negative cannot be processed by the subconscious.)

Only occasionally do we truly consciously override our subconscious mind and decide on a different course of action. This is usually accompanied by some discomfort, increased energy and stress.

The subconscious mind learns very quickly from what we do and develops patterns of behaviour that we call habits—repetitive and reinforcing thoughts and actions that become second nature.

The subconscious also learns our attitude towards things, how we approach issues and subjects, what our beliefs are, based on the information we have hitherto absorbed and filtered, and what expectations we generally have, again based on our experience and the information we have gleaned from all sources.

As these habits become ingrained, they become more difficult and take longer to shift or change. They become automatic.

As we become unconsciously competent it is easy for us to rely on these habits and to act automatically without much additional thought or mindfulness.

There is, of course, great value in this. It is vital for most of the everyday actions we have already described and it keeps us sane and operating efficiently.

If we did not have such automatic habits, we would be having to learn everything as if it was new each time, which would be mind-destroying as well as exhausting.

But our habits have their disadvantages and risks too and our habits, attitudes, beliefs and expectations can also be less than beneficial.

They may, over the course of time, have become either too risky or too risk averse, too bold or too timid, too aggressive or not aggressive enough, based on real-time information or out-of-date assumptions.

When circumstances change or evolve, as they inevitably do, or when faced with entirely new events or challenges and we need to make different decisions or judgments or change course altogether, we may simply and lazily rely on the information conveniently stored in our subconscious mind. We may not take the trouble to stop and think properly and drift into an inappropriate or even disastrous decision, based on previous but now no longer relevant experience.

If we sometimes wonder why we keep making the same mistakes or getting the same results, the cause may be right there. We are not taking the trouble to properly assess our situation and are relying too much on our subconscious mind to direct us based on previous information. Unfortunately, the subconscious does not always have the right data to do this well. And so we keep making the same errors. A description of insanity is 'doing the same thing and expecting a different result', and yet that is what we keep doing.

The information we hold in our subconscious may be entirely inappropriate or wrong (GIGO =

garbage in, garbage out) thus ensuring an automatically generated erroneous response.

We should also ask. How did the information that we hold in our subconscious get there in the first place? Who put it there? Was it the result of careful study or experience or wise counsel? Or was it what we read in a paper or magazine, inherited from the views of our parents, heard from friends or saw on social media?

And how do we know the information is valid anyway?

We don't! And yet we rely on it to make our decisions.

There is the case of the young, talented man from a less privileged background, who had the ability and the grades to go to university. He refused the place. When asked why, he said because his parents had said, 'People like us don't go to university. What will our friends say?' The well-known book, film and musical, *Billy Elliot* exposes similar preconceptions.

Our subconscious reverts to its pool of acquired experience every time we plan to do something.

Unless we consciously decide otherwise, and this takes significant effort and energy, our subconscious mind will effectively decide for us. And all this happens without our being aware of it.

Most of the things we do each day, we do sub-consciously and automatically and we become very **predictable** because the pattern is ingrained and automatic and others can perceive our behaviour patterns easily because they have first-hand experience of them and may well have been their victim. The expression 'reading someone like a book' is a reflection of this predictability.

If we have developed the habit of being on time for appointments or engagements, this becomes very predictable (and vice versa, of course!). So if we are on time for an engagement and we think we're running late, we feel uncomfortable and stressed, our energy and body temperature rises and we automatically speed up.

Our subconscious mind is aware that, given current behaviour, we're going to be late and is activating our bodily responses. The **dissonance** that our subconscious mind feels is translated into a physical response of increased heat and energy.

Our subconscious mind has acquired this behaviour over time and assumes this is how we want to be. It pushes us in the direction it thinks we want to go.

In the case of the person who has acquired the habit of always being late, there is no such dissonance and thus no heat, energy or stress created since none are needed as the subconscious assumes being late is okay, because it always has been for this particular person.

Changing such a habit or any habit is difficult precisely because it entails retraining ourselves; that is, **retraining our subconscious** to a new way of thinking, behaving and acting, changing practices that have been second nature for years.

Changing habits cannot be done quickly either.

It requires time, thought, imagination, vision, energy, goals, repetition and determination.

New Year's resolutions rarely last further than the 2nd of January precisely because these steps have not been properly considered, let alone correctly set up. The chances of success are negligible.

Let's come back to baby. Her subconscious mind becomes attuned very quickly to what happens under different situations. She (her subconscious) learns quickly that positive things happen when she cries. Her subconscious has stored this information and it comes helpfully to the surface anytime something is needed.

If we as parents do not take the opportunity early on to influence baby's subconscious, by, for example, establishing systematic routines for sleep, feeding and play, which her subconscious then stores for future reference (a positive habit), then baby's subconscious will simply assume that it's fine to cry anytime, anyway, anyplace because it always gets results.

And a habit will quickly become ingrained that is not desirable, as many unwary parents have discovered!

It can be very frustrating and stressful for parents and is not healthy for anyone. It becomes even more negative for baby too, whose subconscious picks up the emotions of its parents without being able to process them.

What began as instant gratification and a source of happiness for baby, has become a problem for baby and parents.

So establishing, early, a coherent, stable and regular pattern of behaviour that is beneficial and healthy, as well as caring and warm, filled with cuddles, play and loving attention is a dynamic way of creating an environment of harmony and happiness.

This is then positively stored in our baby's subconscious, as well, let's not forget, as that of parents (and grandparents!).

Habits, attitudes, beliefs and expectations

All this holds equally true for our children as they grow up. They need to be encouraged to develop good habits early—a task that requires kindness, patience and firmness—so that they can store these in their subconscious mind whereupon they become automatic.

Whenever a situation then occurs where they need to make a decision, armed with their good habits, their subconscious will help them make the right choice.

This applies to almost anything they do: being polite, being kind, being positive, smiling, having good manners, doing their homework, crossing the street when the green man lights up, playing nicely with siblings and friends, giving and receiving hugs.

If they can develop the habit of doing these things, so that their actions are natural and an intrinsic part of who they are, then they will have a much greater chance of being happy and creating happiness for those around them.

Life, of course, is not always blissful. Nor should it be! Life, like fate, happens and negative, sad, difficult, dangerous, unfortunate events can and will occur.

*It is not so much what happens to us
that matters but how we deal with it.*

Armed, however, with good habits, the right attitude, a clear philosophy of life and inner strength, as well as appropriate skills, we are much better equipped to handle both good and bad things.

Life is either an exciting adventure or nothing.
Helen Keller

Helen Keller became blind, deaf and dumb when she was nineteen months old as a result of an acute illness, yet lived a magnificent and full life helping and inspiring others, learning to ride, chairing societies and enjoying life to the full.

She was the first deaf-blind person to earn a Bachelor of Arts degree and became an author, political activist and lecturer.

How often have we met or heard of people with serious problems, illnesses or disabilities who are nevertheless positive, energetic, cheerful, helpful, caring and, yes, exude happiness?

At the other extreme, how often have we met people who would appear on the surface to have every advantage, blessing and opportunity, yet who, nevertheless are consistently miserable, envious, depressed, depressing and unhappy?

In the case of Helen Keller, she was determined, from a very early age, to find a way to communicate and break through her almost total isolation. In this she was brilliantly helped by the wonderful Anne Sullivan who coached, encouraged and inspired her with immense patience. The habits of determination, drive and resilience were instilled from the start with remarkable success.

In the sorry case of the person with everything but who continually moans and complains, no such early habits were instilled.

On the contrary, such behaviour is most likely the result of parental neglect, compensated by guilty acquiescence, giving way to any and all demands for the sake of peace and thus helping to instil a habit that will persist into adulthood, unless seriously addressed.

Not only will this attitude have damaged the prospect of a happy life, it will also have damaged the likelihood of a successful one. Who wants to hire someone who moans and complains, blames others when things go wrong and is consistently miserable?

Instilling or acquiring new good habits always requires time, patience, resilience, desire and effort. It requires constant **repetition** so as to create a new way of life that becomes an automatic response.

When force of circumstance upsets your equanimity, lose no time in recovering your self-control and do not remain out of tune longer than you can help. Habitual recurrence to the harmony will increase your mastery of it.
Marcus Aurelius

Personal, quality time needs to be spent with our child in a caring and positive environment. This is often very difficult for working or single parents. If affordable, a good childcare professional, or nursery, working in tandem with the parents can be of significant help.

And even with the greatest efforts of kind and caring parents, it can be very trying and frustrating. What parent has not had to cope with the 'terrible twos', when our child is learning, subconsciously, to develop her own autonomy and, in the process, refusing to co-operate on practically anything?

Extreme patience is required as well as a clear understanding between the parents working together as to what is and is not acceptable or negotiable.

This stage soon passes, to be replaced by new and different challenges.

Our child learns to take initiatives (three to six years) and seeks the approval of peers. She becomes industrious (six to eleven years) wanting to achieve school goals successfully. Then comes a tough period when she develops her identity (twelve to eighteen years) as puberty affects how she sees herself and the world and seeks to discover who she really is.

During this time, as parents we are aware that we seem to spend significant time saying 'no' to our child as she experiments and seeks to discover new things.

Here comes another opportunity to learn something useful:

Research has shown that parents say nineteen times 'no' for every time they say 'yes.'

In addition, when a child does something wrong parents sometimes *criticize the child* directly, not least if the negative behaviour happens frequently—which it will!

Parents often also assume that if a child does not show promise in any particular activity, it means the child must somehow be 'bad' at it and *always will be.*

Nothing could be further from the truth of course, and, in most cases, such judgments are made much too soon and at much too young an age to have any validity whatsoever.

But these judgments, often spoken out loud or implied by someone whose opinion they treasure, affect the child and her subconscious, damage her self-esteem and limit her expectations of herself.

The effect is often much greater than the parent either felt or intended. An unintended slight, casually delivered by a parent and not intended seriously, can nevertheless deeply hurt our child.

It has been found, with adults undergoing be-havioural coaching, that such an off-hand slight, uttered carelessly to them many years before by an unwary parent, was the cause of anxiety and trauma at a later date.

We need to be exceptionally careful about the words we use.

Small wonder that children frequently grow up with negative thoughts about themselves and the world. This colours their attitude, beliefs and expecta-tions about themselves and the world they live in.

It also impedes their learning and development and discourages them from taking initiatives, trying new things, exploring possibilities, in case they should fail and hence disappoint.

In our coaching, we have frequently come across situations where expectations are raised too high too soon, with the result that the child is set up to fail through no fault of her own. She then risks becoming dependent on others, feeling guilty that she is not good enough and inferior compared with her schoolmates.

At the other end of the spectrum, parents sometimes attribute skills and competences to their child that they simply don't yet have. This instils in our child's subconscious the idea that they are much better than they actually are with the result that their minds are closed to learning, because they believe they already know.

And when reality eventually happens, they are in for a shock and experience exactly the same, if not an even higher, sense of failure.

In order to help our child move from a world of instant gratification to one of achievement, here are various key learnings:

1. **Say and especially show you love your child frequently. Avoid criticizing her directly. It is her behaviour you do not love, not her.**

Parents love their children and always will. If the child thinks that her parents do not love her—and say so in frustration—they will, at the very least, damage her self-esteem.

It is not the child that should be criticized, but the behaviour. Say instead: 'I love you, and always will, but *I do not like this behaviour*. It is not worthy of you because *I know you are capable of doing better.*'

2. Role model the behaviour you want.

It seems obvious, but children need role models and the most obvious and best one should be the parent. Nobody is perfect or needs to be, but if we want our child to behave in a certain way, we need to show them the way and do this consistently. If we do the opposite, we should hardly be surprised at the result.

3. Make children responsible for their actions and decisions. Children given responsibility usually act responsibly.

Children are very good at taking on responsibilities when encouraged to do so. They like being responsible for something and thrive on it. They are also much happier and more motivated, as we all are, when the decision is theirs and they are in control.

When the opportunity arises, or when they seek permission to do something, ask them *what they think they should do* and wait for a reply.

If whatever it is they wish to do is positive or helpful, all well and good. If it isn't, start over by asking what they would like to do that would be positive as *you want to treat them as grown-ups*, which means they will be in charge.

This turns the situation around and instead of the parent having to come up with ideas and solutions, the child has to do the thinking work and, in so doing, also learns to think for herself.

At times, this will lead to some frustrations, especially for the older child, adolescent (or adult!) who may say 'tell me what I should do' when they should be able to work it out for themselves.

It is almost as though they do not wish to take responsibility for their own actions, preferring to have the option to blame someone else if things don't work out later.

Resist the temptation to tell them what to do.

The correct reply is 'I know what I would probably do if it was me, but it's not me, it's you. It's your life and it's your responsibility to make that decision. No one can or should make it for you. What I can do is show you what to consider in making that decision, *if you want.*'

Again the responsibility is shifted back and forces them to think while reducing dependency and encouraging self-confidence.

That does not mean that parents should not make suggestions. Of course they should. But there is a way of doing this that can provide helpful information rather than being somewhat manipulative, which our children will detect immediately.

Children like to be like their older siblings and friends and, if so, we should help them, gently and carefully, to achieve just that, while being vigilant about allowing one child more favours than another or imposing a younger child on older siblings.

By asking questions calmly and carefully, a sensible action plan can be arrived at that has the buy-in of child and parent. It is amazing the extent to which this can make life easier all round.

What should one do about laptops and electronic games?

Computer games can be fun and come under the category of instant gratification. Like all instant gratification, it provides a definitive happiness fix and buzz, but one that is likely to be shallow and short-lived. It requires frequent topping-up and becomes time consuming and time wasting. The risks are the same for children as for adults. In limited doses, it can be relaxing and fun. In more extensive doses, it is highly damaging.

Not only does it waste time that could be better employed doing other things, it is also essentially unsocial, even anti-social. Looking at an electronic screen for a long time is also unhealthy in its effects on the eyes and brain and can impede sleep.

Because it can be so addictive, children (and adults) generally find it hard to limit themselves and this becomes another less helpful habit.

It is also clear that such habits are carried into adolescence with worrying effects. Who has not seen, in a café or fast food outlet, a table of adolescents all looking at or playing with their smart phones and hardly ever looking up, let alone indulging in conversation?

We need to instil new habits **early on** by establishing rules, time plans for when to use or not use electronic media and encouragement to develop alternative more constructive activities, such as games, a love of books, cooking, and so on.

Above all, we need to get children to the point quickly where they understand **why** they need to limit their time and do so out of their **own free will**.

Their own strength of character should be gently encouraged and applauded and the benefit of having their own mind needs to be developed.

These positive habits will also act as a valuable safeguard to them when peer pressures mount as they grow up, which they will with a vengeance.

By having strong values, they will be much better equipped to handle the enormous pressures and stresses that they will face as adolescents and have the strength of character not be swayed or drift mindlessly with the herd.

And if their relationship with their parents is such that they are comfortable and happy to talk through their worries and fears in an open **non-judgmental environment before they become real problems**, so much the better. Parents need to make themselves **accessible and good listeners**—major skills in themselves.

It is the nature of the wise to resist pleasures,
but the foolish to be a slave to them.
Epictetus

In an age of conspicuous and mass consumption, it is all too easy to lose sight of what we truly need, as opposed to what we are told, on a daily basis, that we should have for our happiness—the latest gadget or fashion item, the latest thing that will transform us instantly into the person we really should be.

The built-in obsolescence, the beautiful images, the invitation to a dream, the peer pressure, the constant bombardment of advice on how to be up-to-date and not left behind are massive temptations for instant gratification and designed to be so. But do we really need any of them?

If there were **no other people to impress**, would we really make the same material choices we make? Would we live in the same house, have the same car, wear the same clothes and buy the same gadgets? Would we be so quick in allowing materialism to overcome spiritualism quite so easily and completely?

Wealth consists not in having great possessions, but in having few wants.

Where do our attitudes, beliefs and expectations come from?

As with our habits, they all come from our own lived experience of the world, from our approach to life in general and from the say-so of others.

Do any of our attitudes, beliefs and expectations represent the truth? The answer is they represent the truth **only as we believe it to be, or as we have been led to believe it to be, not as it really is.**

By attitude we mean the way we approach an issue. Do we generally have an attitude of openness to ideas and suggestions or do we approach issues more sceptically? This can be changed fairly rapidly.

By beliefs we mean the things we hold to be true, our acceptance and confidence that something exists or is absolute, especially when there is no proof. This takes longer to change.

By expectations we mean the assumptions we make about likely outcomes. This will be conditioned by the degree to which we view the world optimistically or pessimistically. This can be changed fairly quickly.

Take our child: if she is told she is 'no good' at sport, maths, singing, playing the piano or whatever, this is what her subconscious mind will believe. It will become a predominant belief for her—however erroneous that may be. Whenever an opportunity then arises to partake in the activity, she will be reluctant, shy away from trying and avoid it, because she believes she will not succeed. And that belief determines the outcome.

She has been conditioned to fail because that is what she believes. It is the truth as she sees it. It becomes a self-fulfilling prophesy.

Just as with our habits, attitudes to life, beliefs about possibilities and expectations about results are all established early on and are built on as we grow.

Nothing has a stronger influence psychologically on their environment and especially on their children than the unlived life of the parent.
Carl Jung

If we as parents are pessimistic or cynical about the world, fearful about trying anything lest we fail, closed about our environment and the different ways people lead their lives, always expecting the worst, we can expect these to become the attitudes, beliefs and expectations of our children.

Allow children the opportunity to control their own stories by giving them plenty of scope for stimulating their imagination by creating opportunities for them to try new things. Be gentle with their ideas. Allow and encourage them to dream big thoughts.

I have spread my dreams under your feet;
Tread softly because you tread upon my dreams.
W B Yeats

Encourage them to persevere when they don't immediately succeed to develop resilience in a positive environment. Guide them gently along the way, at their request. Celebrate their successes.

Never, ever, ever accept that a child is a lost cause. They all have many abilities and talents. It is just a question of finding which ones they enjoy best, encouraging them with a wide range of options and helping their development.

Take, for example, the case of the youngster with the turbulent childhood whose school reports were damning—'certainly on the road to failure ... hopeless ... rather a clown in class ... wasting other pupils' time.' He was then looked after by his uncle and aunt who encouraged him to read short stories, stimulated his interest in crossword puzzles and music, bought him a mouth organ, gave him a loving home. That was John Lennon.

Or consider the case of the self-taught high school drop-out, considered 'lazy, slow and dreamy', who failed the entrance exam to the Swiss Federal Polytechnic in Zurich, failed to reach the required standard in most subjects other than physics and maths, where he was encouraged, stimulated and inspired by perceptive and caring teachers. That was Albert Einstein.

How about the case of the high school student judged by his teachers to be 'turbulent, quarrelsome, disobedient and unbearable' until given clear responsibility and encouragement in the army. That was Charles de Gaulle.

And what about Winston Churchill, who had an unhappy childhood, a poor relationship with his father, was the pupil with the lowest grades in the lowest class, left school early and only passed the exams to the Royal Military College at the third attempt.

He was recognized there as being very bright, having exceptional courage, great English language and oratorical skills, enormous energy and considerable strength of purpose. He went on to be voted one of the greatest Britons of all time.

As our case studies grew into adults and were helped to acquire and respond to responsibility, they decided on their own careers. Some did so by the force of their personalities, but most were allowed and encouraged in their vocations and activities by mentors and teachers.

In the business world, it's called empowerment. It means allowing employees to be self-directed rather than instructed, motivated rather than depressed, responsible rather than dependent and enabled to grow and flourish rather than stultify.

Studies have shown conclusively that companies where employees feel engaged, that is who feel they are truly part of the organization they work in, share similar positive values, feel empowered and appreciated, are indeed statistically more successful. Hence the growing popularity of engagement studies by enlightened companies and organizations to measure this aspect, track progress and make changes where necessary.

Employees are 'enabled' to exercise their own responsibilities and, as a result, have more success in a more harmonious environment.

As they grow and develop, it is likely they will wish to leave their organization to progress their careers elsewhere.

Enlightened employers will recognize this as a positive thing and the result of the company's excellent mentoring in an environment that encourages personal growth.

They will realize that the fact that their employees are sought by other companies is a reflection of their own excellence in developing talent, factors that will make the company even more desirable to the most aspiring and capable of the next generation of professionals, thus perpetuating a virtuous cycle!

Here comes another essential learning opportunity:

We are what we think.
Controlling our 'self-talk' is critical.

While we need to be careful about where our habits, attitudes, beliefs and expectations come from and who put them there, we also need to be mindful of **how we talk to ourselves**, our self-talk, which is directly related to them.

Self-talk is that little voice that is constantly chattering away inside our head. We sometimes hear it clearly and sometimes it is just mumbling away indistinctly, although we know the gist of what it is saying. Like our subconscious, it is directing our thoughts and our actions.

When we encounter something or someone, or even as we pass the time of day, our self-talk is chatting to us: 'I really like this.' 'This is so exciting!' 'What a stupid remark!' 'Why doesn't he move over into the slow lane?'

Earlier we saw how that little voice persuaded us to say something we had not intended to say. *That was our self-talk overriding our conscious mind.*

Self-talk is our subconscious mind reflecting back to us the habits, attitudes, beliefs and expectations that we have created over our lifetime.

Be mindful of what it is saying to you.

It is dictating your thoughts and your thoughts dictate your actions. Remember the following phrases: **As I think, I am. We are what we think. Our intentions determine our future.**

If we think negative thoughts, that's how we'll be. If we believe the world is an inimical place, we'll be miserable. If we think the world owes us a living, we'll simply complain when we don't get our way. If we complain, we are in effect blaming others for our predicament.

If we think everyone else is to blame for our misfortune, we will shift responsibility to 'others', whoever these others may be and sit back and do nothing. The negative spiral will continue unchecked. This is negative energy and we lose inner strength and power every time.

If, on the other hand, we believe that it is possible to succeed, that we can take actions to improve any given situation, that we are positive and optimistic about outcomes and are thus open to solutions, that is how we will behave. If we believe that, for every situation we encounter, there is positive learning to be gained and a thoughtful and loving response to be given, then we create positive energy and we gain inner strength and power.

Whenever we feel a little down or uncomfortable or unhappy about something, there is a reason. We need to examine that reason carefully in order to find the right response and gain benefit rather than the opposite.

Suppose we have just been with friends in a social situation, and we come away feeling a little negative, we have to ask ourselves very honestly and dispassionately why. Was it something someone said or did that made us feel inadequate, angry, overlooked, silly, aggrieved, resentful or belittled? Was it that we made a comment we felt was important but was dismissed? Was it how we were 'judged' by our friends?

Close and careful examination of these emotions will lead us to discover what it was that triggered our negative response. When we discover what it was, and, say, we conclude that we heard a comment that we felt dismissed something we had said without any consideration, we discover that our discomfort is the result of feeling resentful about having been ignored.

What should our reaction be?

On the one hand, we can continue to feel aggrieved and unhappy, resentful, disappointed, even angry and vengeful. 'How could my friend have so dismissed me?' 'What sort of a friend would do this?' 'This can't be a true friend.' 'We're clearly very different.' 'Maybe I should drop this friendship?'

Or we can learn from this, and all future encounters, by asking ourselves what would be a wiser, more mature, more loving response, rather than our automatic, angry one. Is our friend not entitled to her views, even negative ones? Could we have expressed the thought differently? Or maybe not at all? Isn't our friendship greater than this? Have I not done exactly the same thing on other occasions? Maybe this wasn't the right occasion anyway to introduce this thought? Is it healthy to maintain this negative energy? And for what purpose? Who really cares other than me? Is it good to allow our perception of the motives or actions of others to control our emotions?

Forgiving is a much more positive force for happiness. Letting go is so much more relieving. Both of these enhance our inner strength.

Viewing occasions when we feel low with a response based on wisdom and compassion rather than anger and hurt creates much more positive energy and happiness.

Which response would we rather have?

If we can make this response a behaviour that is second nature to us, it will lead to the right response and the right action. The right action will lead to a commitment to view life and our universe in a different and more positive way, and commitment will lead to transformed results.

Until one is committed, there is hesitancy,
the chance to draw back, always ineffectiveness.
Concerning all acts of initiative (or creation),
there is one elementary truth, the ignorance of
which kills countless ideas and splendid plans:
that the moment one definitely commits oneself,
then Providence moves too.
W H Murray

It is remarkable how success breeds success, as long as we have the persistence, resilience and commitment to take appropriate and wise action, not blindly but in an attitude of openness to constructive suggestions.

Using imagination to change the picture

What to do if you catch your self-talk muttering negative thoughts:

1. **Stop the negative thought right there!**
2. **Confront your thought directly.**
3. **Make the decision to alter it and use your imagination to change the picture.**

Consider the following: the cyclist is riding too slowly ahead of you and you're in your car becoming increasingly frustrated because you can't overtake (but might be tempted to with dangerous consequences).

Your self-talk becomes negative and says to you: 'Why can't he move over or speed up?' 'Why can't he just steer into the side so I can get by?' 'Cyclists are such a menace.' 'He's holding up the entire traffic!'

Now, stop the negative thoughts dead!

Use your imagination to change the picture by visualizing something different and more positive.

For example, in the case of being slowed down by the cyclist, change the picture and **visualize this instead: that cyclist could be my son, my daughter or my friend.**

Say to yourself: 'As a responsible, loving and moral person, my duty is to protect them absolutely.'

If it were my own child on the bike, my self-talk would be very different and so would my behaviour and actions.

By changing the picture, my self-talk shifts from a negative, irritated, potentially dangerous attitude, to one that is more caring and patient—and a lot safer. If I do this each time I am confronted with such a situation, my anxiety reduces and I behave in a calmer, more considered manner. By taking decisions and making choices based on wisdom and love, rather than anger and resentment, I gain inner strength. The more I do this, the easier it gets and, in time, it becomes second nature and a much happier way to live.

This essentially Stoic method applies to any of our anxieties, stresses and fears and works equally well with all of them.

It is a form of exposure therapy, which is arguably the best scientifically supported technique in psychotherapy.

It takes some practice and repetition. Exercise by observing behaviour first in mildly stressful situations and deliberately alter the picture. The more we practise, the easier it becomes and positive results will inevitably follow.

We can create a new, healthier, safer, calmer habit.

Take away thy opinion, and then there is taken away the complaint, "I have been harmed." Take away the complaint "I have been harmed," and the harm is taken away.
Marcus Aurelius

Overriding our self-talk and changing the picture is relevant also to collective environments, where group dynamics take over and collective lemming-like behaviours then occur.

Collective self-talk, as in a business or any wider environment, is called rumour or post-truth. This can be highly damaging as it promulgates falsehoods and stimulates individual untruthful self-talk and all the emotions that go with that.

When situations are ambiguous or uncertain and there is an absence of official information or fact, people make it up—they invent the 'facts'. And they will usually make them up negatively. The really bad news is that life is always ambiguous, so we are constantly bombarded by half-truths and opinion masquerading as fact.

Everything we hear is an opinion, not a fact.
Everything we see is a perspective, not the truth.

Because all is opinion,
everything is what you suppose it to be.
Marcus Aurelius

The only way to counter this negativity is to avoid believing rumours—or, worse still, condoning or agreeing with them.

In the same way that we need to question our self-talk and override it when it is clearly pointing in the wrong direction, so too we have to recognize when rumour is simply collective self-talk and not based on factual information.

Our self-talk, like collective self-talk, reflects all the prejudices we have acquired. Be mindful of that. Listen carefully to what you're saying to yourself. Then change the picture if it isn't what you want.

Remember too that it is not the event or person that is the cause of our anxiety or frustration, it is the view we ourselves are taking of them, the view that our self-talk is expressing, that is causing the problem.

Man is disturbed not by things,
but by the views he takes of them.
Epictetus

When we allow ourselves to be irritated, angry or anxious about events or people, we need to remember that it is not the event itself or the person that is the irritant—they are either neutral or totally indifferent—it is **our own internal image, our own judgment**, that is the cause. If we change the internal picture, our judgment will change too.

If you are pained by external things,
it is not they that disturb you, but
your own judgment of them. And it is in
your power to wipe out that judgment now.
Marcus Aurelius

How often have we pre-judged someone, believing them to be boring or obnoxious, only to find, when we get to know them, that they are anything but our previous assumption of them? We created a view in our mind that was completely false and it had disturbed us quite unnecessarily.

Had we started out with a more open mind and not allowed our *pre*-judgment, or prejudice, to dictate our self-talk, we would have discovered the positives sooner.

How many other times have we allowed our prejudices to limit our enjoyment of the world and our happiness?

'An unexamined life is not worth living,' said Socrates, and Plato believed that happiness comes from taking positive, moral decisions and actions.

Learning to control our self-talk is key to *examining* our mind, creating more positive pictures, adjusting our viewpoint and stimulating the opportunity for happiness.

Use a quiet moment to stop and **listen** to what your self-talk is saying to you. Is it positive or negative, sarcastic or complimentary, uplifting or depressing, reasonable or excessive? See if you can detect a pattern.

If you are not satisfied with what you find, catch your unsatisfactory self-talk next time it arises and make a clear effort to **stop and change it right there**. Replace the negative self-talk with a more positive image and create a new self-talk for yourself.

Consider the following case: Mrs G would frequently burst into tears on routine occasions such as walking the dogs in the park, on shopping trips, or at home in the kitchen or even at dinner parties. She was deeply unhappy, verging on depression.

When asked why, she said she was still in mourning for her mother. When asked how long ago her mother had died, she said some five years before.

What was happening was that when, for example, she took the dogs for a walk in the park, something she used to enjoy doing with her mother, a picture of her mother during her last days would spring up in her mind and she would immediately become very sad, leading to floods of tears.

She loved her mother very much and quite understandably missed her.

In order to start to address the issue, she was asked to take time, at home and on regular occasions to *visualize* her mother, not in her last days but when she was healthy and full of life and to *picture* her happy, laughing and smiling in different situations, especially those special occasions when they were together.

She was asked to do this several times a day and to *look up* while doing so. (It is much more difficult to be sad when looking up.)

After relatively few days, Mrs G said she was feeling much better and after three weeks her unhappiness had dissipated altogether. She still had feelings of sadness, but these were increasingly being replaced with images of happiness.

Reflect regularly on your habits, attitudes, beliefs and expectations. Where did they come from? Who put the ideas there in the first place and are they the right ones for you? Or are they limiting your ability to move forward? Are they creating a prison for you?

The key to our prison is in our own pocket. We have the power and freedom to open it anytime—if we so choose.

We do not need to become chained in Plato's 'cave' unable to perceive a better life, only seeing the shadows, not reality, and condemned to confuse ill-considered beliefs with truth.

Let us have the courage to escape from our prison cave!

Only then can we be in a position to climb up the stairway.

The secret of happiness is freedom.
And the secret to freedom is courage.

THE SECOND STEP:

THE HAPPINESS OF ACHIEVING

We have seen how instant gratification, while providing short-term and rather ephemeral happiness, can quickly become problematic if not set in a sensible context with a modicum of discipline.

Setting a sensible context is the result of considered thought combined with deliberate action to develop a new habit.

Developing a new habit is an act of achievement, as opposed to self-gratification, because it requires effort and energy and, if successful, results in a sense of achievement, which is the *happiness of achieving*.

In the Stoic philosophy, the only two things we can control are our **thoughts** and **actions**. When we want or need to change a habit, we have the opportunity to control both in such a way as to improve our life and happiness.

Changing habits requires patience, self-awareness and some discipline, but the discipline is only required until such time as the new habit has been established—it is no longer needed once the new behaviour has become automatic. It is then much easier.

Creating a new habit can be done in the following way:

1. The first step is to be absolutely clear **what we want to create as a new habit and why** and **write it down**. Committing to paper has the advantage that it cannot be overridden by our subconscious mind. It is there to be seen all the time, whereas just thinking ideas has no lasting value and tomorrow will be another day with another thought and again inaction.

2. The second step is to enumerate and **write down as many reasons as we can gather why we absolutely need to create this new habit,** so as to develop an **overwhelming** case to ourselves that **such a change will be beneficial to us and in our own interest.**

3. The third step is to write or rewrite our new habit **in the present tense and in**

the affirmative (no negatives as the sub-conscious mind, as we now know, cannot process a negative). The fact that it is in the present tense creates a dissonance with the subconscious mind (which says it isn't true) thus creating an energy to either do something to reconcile the new habit with a new reality or go back to the old reality. We also need to **visualize ourselves in the new habit**, remembering the formula I + V x R = NR (Imagination + Visualisation x Repetition = New Reality).

4. The fourth is to **begin immediately** (not tomorrow or next time we have a moment) and read our new commitment morning, noon and night and whenever we feel the need to keep strong (notice the absence of any negative notions of giving up or finding it hard to find the time). If we can, we should link this to a program of short-term goals.

5. The fifth is to **persevere** and maintain steady progress until the new habit has become second nature, whereupon it ceases to become an effort as the subconscious mind reconciles the dissonance and adopts the new state.

Let's take an example.

George is a middle-aged man who has done little exercise in the past twenty years, is overweight, unfit, with high blood pressure and an unhealthy body mass index. He works hard and as soon as he gets home he pours himself a drink, has a meal with a glass (or two) of wine and sits himself in front of the TV until it's time to go to bed, which he does at approximately the same time every weekday.

George would like to do something about this— not least because his medical was rather alarming and his metabolic age was significantly higher than his actual age.

Let's follow the steps.

1. Be clear about the new habit we want to create and why, and then write it down. After a few attempts, George writes: 'I want to be fit in order to be healthy.'

2. Write down as many reasons as possible why this is vital and in our own interest, and create an overwhelming case for change. George writes dozens of reasons, such as, 'I want to see my children (and grandchildren) grow up.' 'I want to feel good about myself.'

'I want to feel alive.' 'I want to feel happy.' 'I want to have more energy.' 'I want to enjoy playing football with my son.' 'I want to be comfortable running a half marathon.' 'I want my family to be proud of me.' 'I want to show myself that I can achieve difficult things.' 'If I don't change, my health, my family, my prospects, my enjoyment of life, my happiness and those of my nearest and dearest will be unhappily affected.'

3. Write our new habit in the present tense and in the affirmative. George writes: 'I AM A FIT AND HEALTHY PERSON!' 'But you're not,' says the subconscious mind, 'so stop messing around and come back to the person you really are!' This is why George's reasons for changing have to be well thought through and persuasive and where visualizing the new state comes in: 'I AM A FIT AND HEALTHY PERSON and, what's more, I can see exactly how I look and feel as a fit, healthy person. That is who I really am.'

4. George reads his statement of commitment several times a day, schedules a program of exercise on a regular basis, signs up with a

personal trainer to start off, has a program of short- and longer-term goals, finds time to exercise during lunch breaks, in the evening after work, before going to work and at weekends, reduces his alcohol consumption to weekends only, reduces his portion sizes and switches to a healthier, reduced-sugar diet.

5. After three months, George is still reading his statement of commitment every day and evening and his progress has been very rapid. He goes regularly to the gym and has had to increase his goals several times as they have mostly been achieved. He enjoys playing football with his son and is much better able to do so as he has more energy and enthusiasm. He is happier at work and at home, has lost weight and his blood pressure is closer to normal. He now experiences what he calls a *joie de vivre*, the happiness to be alive, and he feels good about himself. Above all, the new routine seems now to be quite easy and has become a way of life for him. He has no intention of going back.

George will need to continue to exercise for the rest of his life and may need to enlist the help of a personal trainer from time to time to maintain his enthusiasm and learn new methods.

He has, however, experienced the happiness of achieving.

George is a hypothetical example. He is, however, one that is rooted in real situations and real outcomes, which happen every day.

Keeping physically fit is of course also a wonderful way of feeling happy, not so much because of the adrenaline rush (although that's nice too) but because being fit and healthy allows us to feel good about ourselves, allows us to view life more positively, is better for our health, gives us greater optimism and helps us to see our universe more benignly.

The methodology described above is applicable to any and all circumstances where change is wanted and a new habit is desired.

Look well into thyself; there is a source of strength which will always spring up if thou wilt always look.

The happiness of achieving comes from doing something that requires effort and energy, presents a challenge (however small) and can be shown to have been achieved when completed.

One of the ways of re-establishing confidence in someone who has suffered psychological trauma is to allow them to set small goals for themselves, related to the re-establishment of trust not only in themselves but also in others, and that they can achieve.

In our busy lives, how often do we set out to do any number of things, make arrangements with friends and family, take care of myriad domestic, financial and social imperatives only to find, by the end of the day, we have only done a fraction of them?

We then feel both guilty and bad, and promise to correct this pattern of behaviour, only to do it all over again.

If we ask people, 'How often, on average, do you only speak the truth?' most people will score well above eighty percent and they will be truthful in their answer.

If we now ask them, 'How often do you keep your promises?' the response is much lower.

Promises are, or should be, a **commitment to achieve** with and for ourselves or with and for another.

To the extent that we honour our commitment, we feel a sense of satisfaction and happiness. To the extent that we fail to meet that commitment, not only do we feel unhappy, **we have also psychologically damaged our self-esteem and we lose inner strength**.

> *Always bear in mind that your own resolution to succeed is more important than any other one thing.*
> **Abraham Lincoln**

The importance of self esteem

People with high self-esteem will on average always perform better than people with low self-esteem. Poor self-esteem leads to poor or even negative performance and we are back in the vicious cycle of a bad habit perpetuating itself.

We need to convert the vicious cycle into a virtuous one.

One of the best ways to increase self-esteem is to achieve predetermined goals that have some appropriate level of challenge.

By nature, human beings are motivated by goals and this creates energy and enthusiasm for their completion. Goal-setting is also vital for survival and studies have shown that people in retirement who have goals have a longer life expectancy than those who haven't.

At the same time, we need to be mindful of setting goals that are our own, not those defined by others.

We need to take care not to 'under-live' our potential because of all the past information that has been absorbed in the expectation part of our subconscious.

A good coach is one who sees more potential in an individual than that person, or indeed others, can see themselves. Let's remember the case of Helen Keller and her coach, Anne Sullivan.

The setting and accomplishment of goals, which is the essence of the happiness of achieving, is also the best way of moving out of instant gratification and its attendant risk of stagnation, and building self-esteem—vital to all the next steps on the stairway.

Children, especially between the ages of five and twelve, need to win approval by demonstrating skills and abilities that are valued by their parents, peers and their environment so that they can begin to develop a sense of pride in their accomplishments, positive self-esteem and a positive self-image.

Parents need to reinforce and encourage the initiatives that children suggest and, while allowing some failures to avoid overconfidence and encourage modesty, should celebrate successes where specific skills and competences have been developed and demonstrated. This builds self-esteem.

If our child does not develop such skills she may begin to feel inferior, leading to low self-esteem and a lower ability to experience the happiness of achieving.

In order for children, and adults, to build their self-esteem, and their confidence, they need goals and the wherewithal to achieve them—ambition, determination, energy, drive, focus, resilience, hard work and competence.

If you set yourself to your present task along the path of true reason, with all determination, vigour, and good will: if you admit no distraction, expecting nothing, shirking nothing, but self-content with each present action taken in accordance with nature and a heroic truthfulness in all that you say and mean—then you will lead a good life. And nobody is able to stop you.
Marcus Aurelius

Setting goals

Setting goals which are then met is a valid way of building self-esteem and gaining joy from the happiness of achieving.

The act of changing a habit, as we have seen, is in itself a goal achieved and the methodology has already been explained.

The wider question then arises and must be addressed: what goals should we have? How challenging should they be? How specific or vague? How many should we have? Over what time scale?

What goals?

So let's consider first what the goals might be.

It is often said that a goal or the goals should be SMART or even SMARTER, which stands for Specific (simple, sensible, significant), Measurable (meaningful, motivating), Achievable (agreed, doable), Relevant (reasonable, realistic, resourced, useful), Time bound (with agreed dates for completion), Evaluated and Reviewed.

This is perfectly sound and has been used very frequently, especially in a business environment, to establish **what** is required, **why** it is required, **who** is involved, **where** it takes place, **which** resources are needed and **when** it is to be completed.

It is particularly relevant to the setting of immediate **tasks—once the overall direction of travel has been established.** The need for creative or imaginative solutions is not high (and sometimes positively discouraged) and the context is somewhat narrow.

SMART's uses, then, are limited to specific actions. It doesn't answer the question about what our goals should be.

Establishing a bigger picture first

Establishing our goals is not a trivial exercise, but one that needs to be seen in a much wider context than is usually the case.

If it is our ambition to be millionaires at thirty, or win an Olympic gold medal, or become prime minister or a concert pianist, this will not happen because we 'will' it to, or 'imagine' the outcome sufficiently positively. It will only happen by dint of tremendous sacrifices, hard work, tireless efforts, talent and a lot of good luck!

These sacrifices will affect not only our lives, but the lives of many others. There is no such thing as a single goal because of its ripple effect on other aspects of our life and those of others.

And then, our ambition may not happen at all, or only in part.

If we have just a single, overweening idea or ambition in mind, and it fails, then we are likely to be much less well off than if we had not started. We will also feel disappointed and a failure and, should we have unwisely invested in the idea, a lot less well-off to boot.

Even if we are successful with our single-minded objective, what then? It is said that when Alexander the Great had succeeded in defeating all the kingdoms he could, he wept. There was no one else to conquer.

Our success should be seen also in the context of our sacrifices. What did we miss out on while we were pursuing our goal so ardently? Did we have time for our family? Did we see our children grow up, play their matches, attend their concerts, find quality time for them? What happened to our health with all that stress? What happened to us as human beings?

Or have we simply left behind a string of unhappy relationships, estranged children, broken families and anxiety about the future, while our health has deteriorated?

If we did win an Olympic medal but can now no longer compete as age catches up, which it will inevitably do, what now? How do we conduct the rest of our lives? How do we avoid feeling a sense of depressive emptiness?

True happiness is to enjoy the present, without anxious dependence upon the future, not to amuse ourselves with either hope or fears but to rest satisfied with what we have, which is sufficient, for he that is so wants nothing. The greatest blessings of mankind are within us and within our reach. A wise man is content with his lot, whatever it may be, without wishing for what he has not.

Letting go all else, cling to the following few truths. Remember that man lives only in the present. In this fleeting instant: all the rest of his life is either past and gone, or not yet revealed. This mortal life is a little thing, lived in a little corner of the earth: and little too is the longest fame to come, dependent as it is on a succession of fast-perishing little men who have no knowledge even of their own selves, much less of one long dead and gone.
Marcus Aurelius

These quotations are not, as they might appear, a cynical call for inaction when confronted by impossible achievements.

Rather they are a call to look at who we are, our lives and our goals, in a different way, with more humility and more wisdom. We need to prepare our inner selves in a way that will enable us to face any and all aspects of our external future tasks with equanimity, calm reasoning, an absence of fear and an acceptance that most aspects of life cannot be controlled.

We need to be mindful that chance, fate or luck play a major role in our successes or failures, whatever we might wish to think, and learn to manage the two elements in our lives that are controllable, namely our thoughts and our actions and let go what we cannot control—but desperately try to—namely everything else.

Never let the future disturb you. You will meet it, if you have to, with the same weapons of reason which today arm you against the present.
Marcus Aurelius

Marcus Aurelius and many of his fellow Stoics were very successful people, enjoying wealth, fame, acclaim, power. Marcus Aurelius was considered one of the five greatest Roman emperors. He was a successful leader at a particularly difficult time for an embattled Rome and his greatest legacy is his writings and reflections.

His philosophy was one of simplicity, reason, justice, self-discipline and calm.

Epictetus, a major influence on Marcus Aurelius, was born a slave. He became disabled when his leg was deliberately broken. His passion for philosophy allowed him to get educated and he gained his freedom as a youth. He became an outstanding thinker, speaker and teacher. He lived a simple life, with few possessions, to the age of eighty. Given his origins as a slave, he was able to understand fully that since we are able uniquely to control our own thoughts, and no one can take that away, it follows that we are also uniquely responsible for our actions and should not be anxious about what is not within our power to influence.

If, then, the things which are independent of the will are neither good nor bad, and all things which do depend on the will are within our power, and no man can either take them from us or give them to us, if we do not choose, where is room for anxiety?

Epictetus

They were successful precisely because their lives were founded and grounded on solid inner principles of virtue, reason, ethical training, humility, self-reflection, careful judgment, inner calm and freedom of thought.

The happiness of achieving that they experienced was the result of the philosophical foundations that underlay their decisions and expectations.

Unless, they would say, our goals are founded on solid principles, regularly practiced so as to enable us to learn and grow, then even if we succeed with our goal, we will still be the same person as before, with all our fears and anxieties.

My true self is free. It cannot be contained.

With the benefit of this knowledge we can reset our goals in a different, more holistic context, recognizing that our goals are interdependent.

When establishing our goals, let us look at not just one aspect but many aspects of our lives, so as to establish a more balanced set.

What ambition do we have for our professional, family and social lives, leisure time and hobbies, holidays, our physical and mental health, and our wealth ambitions and retirement needs? It is important to make this list as extensive and relevant as possible, so as to cover all aspects of our life.

1. Create a pie or bar chart that shows what an **ideal** work-life balance would be for each element you consider important to your life and happiness. Pencil in each bar the level of importance you would ideally attribute to it. This will establish the relative position of each element to each other as well as their overall importance. Consult your partner and family.

2. Do the same thing but this time pencil in each bar to the level that it **currently is**.

3. **Compare** the two charts to establish where the differences are.

4. Think carefully about **which** of the differences need to be addressed and **how**.

We now have the basis for establishing a set of goals that correspond more exactly to what we really want and, hopefully, need in our lives. Also, by establishing several goals, if one does not work out, we have more to fall back on.

Which ones can we control ourselves? Which ones can we only partly control? And which ones are entirely outside our control? If any are completely outside our control, we should simply **let them go**.

Each goal then needs to be carefully assessed, written down in the detail that is necessary to ascertain when it has been achieved—what will it look like when achieved—and broken down into manageable pieces with reasonable timescales and clear actions.

We need also to convert our goals into achievements. When it is our responsibility we need to learn how to take decisions wisely and in a timely manner. This requires concentration, courage and decisiveness. Hesitation is a recipe for procrastination and failure.

Concentrate on what you have to do.
Fix your eyes on it. Remind yourself that
your task is to be a good human being ...
Then do it, without hesitation, and speak the
truth as you see it. But with kindness.
With humility. Without hypocrisy.
Marcus Aurelius

At the same time our goals need to be sufficiently **flexible** to allow for inevitable changes to circumstances. Rigid goals, rigidly upheld, are a recipe for failure, as the world in which we live and operate today changes very rapidly with each new technology.

While the **overall direction of travel** needs continuity, individual goals need to reflect reality as it evolves and changes, with all its complexities.

(One of main issues today is that decisions are increasingly rapidly demanded, not least by a restless and insistent public and media, when in fact the issues themselves, for which decisions are required, are often more complex, requiring more time for careful understanding and resolution, before any sensible goals can be set. While 'shooting from the hip' and providing catchy soundbites is quite popular at times, it is a very poor way of establishing meaningful goals, let alone wise decisions.)

None of these matters are easy but then …

… as Seneca wrote: *There is not an easy way from the earth to the stars*, and as Louis Pasteur wrote: *Fortune favours the prepared mind.*

The happiness of achieving provides a level of satisfaction that is clearly deeper, longer lasting and more profound than instant gratification.

Its true value, however, resides in what kind of goals we set ourselves, how we have set them and what impact our goals have on our soul and inner harmony and those around us.

> *As is a tale, so is life: not how long it is,*
> *but how good it is, is what matters.*
> **Seneca**

THE THIRD STEP:
THE HAPPINESS OF GIVING

So far, the achievement of happiness has been predominantly concerned with the self. Instant gratification is about personal happiness based on gratifying one's own wants and mainly about acquiring things, while the happiness of achieving is about succeeding at goals for ourselves.

To the extent, however, that the goals we set ourselves are for the benefit of others, which they will be if they are about improving other people's lives, or about our own self-improvement in order to be better able to make others happy, then we are into the third stage—the happiness of giving.

Studies have shown conclusively that once basic material needs are satisfied (food, home, reasonable financial security) there is little if any relationship between the accumulation of wealth and increased happiness.

Lottery winners have not become significantly happier—often the opposite has been the case—and extremely wealthy people are not significantly happier either. Their wealth often brings in its wake issues of anxiety, health, stress, family discord, social discord and excessive behaviour.

There is, however, a strong relationship between giving and happiness.

> ***The heart that gives, gathers.***
> **Old English proverb**

Studies have shown that people who volunteer and help others enjoy better psychological health. The benefits to mental health are said to be at least as great if not greater than attending religious services or taking up exercise.

Studies have also shown that when people whose basic material needs are satisfied were given money, they were happier spending it on others than on themselves. These kinds of financial contribution can be in many forms such as simple charitable giving to setting up charities to look after those in need.

But giving does not have to entail money at all. Giving of one's talents or one's time, giving advice, support and encouragement, giving as an act of kindness, giving shared laughter and giving love are all acts of giving.

No one has ever become poor by giving.

The happiness derived from these are more than feeling good about oneself but closely related to a **powerful sense of connection and empathy** to others, engendering a more intense feeling of happiness.

Before giving, the mind of the giver is happy;
while giving, the mind of the giver
is made peaceful; and having given,
the mind of the giver is uplifted.

Generosity is about caring for others by being unselfish and thoughtful, not only with our money but also with our time. It is a positive behaviour aimed at enhancing someone else's happiness.

The opposite of generosity is 'being mean' which is essentially selfish in that the giver is thinking much more of himself and the negative impact of the gift on him rather than the happiness of the recipient.

Being generous, altruistic, giving time and energy helping others, volunteering or simply giving of oneself by being kind, compassionate, considerate and thoughtful will enhance well-being and happiness. It will also enhance inner strength.

> *It was our belief that the love of*
> *possessions is a weakness to be overcome.*
> *Children must learn early the beauty of*
> *generosity. They are taught to give what*
> *they prize most, that they may taste*
> *the happiness of giving ...*
> **Charles Alexander Eastman, also known as Ohiyesa**

Socrates and Seneca do not directly address the concept of giving. But their philosophy arrives at the same conclusion.

The argument goes like this. If a person examines life carefully, they will learn and attain over time a level of knowledge and gain wisdom. Knowledge and wisdom lead to virtue. Knowledge and wisdom, and hence virtue, must be sought before private interests and are the means by which ethical actions and decisions are made. Virtue is good and good is defined as being beneficial to others.

'Beneficial to others' includes any kind of help offered to others including finance, safety, health, well-being, advice, teaching, educating, advising, caring, consoling, influencing in someone's favour and speaking on someone's behalf.

In effect, the virtuous person will naturally want to do what benefits others, which includes all aspects of giving.

As has already been implied, giving does not have to be material. It takes many forms, but must be done **freely** and never grudgingly.

For something to count as a benefit, it must be given because that is what the giver wants to do and has chosen to do of their own free will. No other motives must accompany the act of generosity.

Similarly, it must also be something that is not perceived by the receiver as a burden, an unwanted tie or the creation of a dependence or obligation.

There is an art or style to both giving and receiving. It is something that should be done without fanfare or fuss purely for the joy it brings to both parties. It applies to both the giver and the receiver.

It is not uncommon for people who are givers to find it hard to be receivers. They are happy to give compliments, advice, help and support but find it difficult to receive or to be as gracious when receiving.

It is as if they feel they are not worthy of this treatment, partly out of a sense of modesty, partly because they feel they have somehow not deserved the praise or support and partly because they feel they should not need praise or help.

Giving and taking should be seen as part of the same process, and the same respect needs to be shown by both parties

To brush off the compliment is to dishonour, however unwittingly, the giver and make them feel confused, and perhaps unhappy.

A simple, honest 'thank you' will often suffice, but it is surprising how often such an effective acknowledgement is forgotten.

Every relationship is one of give and take. Giving engenders receiving and receiving engenders giving. ... In reality ... giving and receiving are different aspects of the flow of energy in the universe. ... Practicing the Law of Giving is actually very simple: if you want joy, give joy to others; if you want love, learn to give love; if you want attention and appreciation, learn to give attention and appreciation ...
Deepak Chopra

Giving and receiving need to be in balance.

If the receiver is unable to receive or to respond with gratitude or happiness but rather feels guilty or powerless, then balance cannot be achieved and continuing to give only makes the situation worse.

Under such circumstances, giving alone will lead to unhappiness. Receiving, just as giving, needs to be learnt. It requires dignity and grace as it is our response to what others are giving of themselves to us.

What does one person give to another?
He gives of himself, of the most precious he has,
he gives of his life. This does not necessarily
mean that he sacrifices his life for the other
— but that he gives him of that which is alive
in him; he gives him of his joy, of his interest,
of his understanding, of his knowledge, of his
humour, of his sadness — of all expressions and
manifestations of that which is alive in him.
In thus giving of his life, he enriches the other
person, he enhances the other's sense of aliveness
by enhancing his own sense of aliveness. He
does not give in order to receive; giving is in
itself exquisite joy. But in giving he cannot help
bringing something to life in the other person,

and this which is brought to life reflects back to him; in truly giving, he cannot help receiving that which is given back to him. Giving implies to make the other person a giver also and they both share in the joy of what they have brought to life. In the act of giving something is born, and both persons involved are grateful for the life that is born for both of them.
Erich Fromm

The happiness of giving is a universal happiness in that it transcends all cultures and creeds and is a fundamental step towards universal harmony.

Gentleness, self-sacrifice and generosity are the exclusive possession of no one race or religion.
Mahatma Gandhi

THE FOURTH STEP:
THE HAPPINESS OF RELATIONSHIPS

The happiness of relationships is all about giving and receiving, with the added notion of deep personal, emotional, physical and spiritual love for others.

In this respect, it builds on the happiness of giving and adds an extra dimension. Strong relationships are joyful precisely because they are what is best in human nature, and human beings are social beings who depend and thrive on positive social interactions. The closer and genuinely more heartfelt these interactions, the deeper the connection and the greater the level of happiness.

Such connections are very special and quite rare. They take time and patience to develop and require understanding, empathy, common values and an intimately shared sense of what matters in life and in the world.

Above all they require a deep desire to care, to cherish the other person unconditionally and to uplift them whenever possible.

To achieve this level of connection in any relationship is difficult, and there are many potential obstacles.

These need to be understood in order to be overcome.

In the paragraphs below, we examine a number of key issues.

Relationships need symmetry

Relationships need to be in balance and harmonious if they are to succeed.

A relationship is 'symmetrical' when each is giving and taking in equal measure and the relationship is based on sound *shared* values. Then it has the potential to lead to the wonderful happiness that comes when one soul discovers and appreciates another.

Friendship arises out of mere companionship when two or more companions discover that they have in common some insight or interest or even taste which the

others do not share and which, till that moment,
each believed to be his unique treasure (or
burden). The typical expression of opening
friendship would be something like,
"What? You too? I thought I was the only one."
CS Lewis

A symmetrical relationship is one of mutual trust, peace, calm, respect, honour, freedom and love, where each feels the same for the other and contributes wholeheartedly to the relationship.

Nothing is unsaid. There are no elephants in the room that no one wants to address. It is okay to raise anything since the approach to any issue is to find a sensible solution together—rather than find fault or to judge.

Differences of views and opinions are aired openly and easily with the objective of finding common, acceptable solutions or just agreeing to disagree, which is fine too. There is no sense of 'winning' or 'losing' since both gain. Even heated arguments result in hugs and laughter.

Good relationships are not about being in agreement about everything. They are about acceptance, tolerance, compassion, respect, reverence and caring.

Relationships are based on four principles: respect, understanding, acceptance and appreciation.
Mahatma Gandhi

Symmetrical relationships happen with partners, friends, siblings and family, or within associations, groups and teams and are encompassed within the five words for love that the Ancient Greeks used, especially *philia*.

On the other hand, some relationships are or can become 'asymmetrical', that is to say one partner or friend is giving much more, or **feels or believes** they are giving much more to the relationship than the other.

This can also occur when the needs of one (whether for reassurance or control) are very different or more intense than the needs of the other.

Or when the partners, not sharing the same values or with different approaches to life or to people, begin to feel they are not on the same wavelength and talk at cross purposes.

Asymmetry also arises when the quality of listening skills is sadly lacking or when there is an absence of true caring and compassion.

Or when there is a high degree of judgment, based, as it must inevitably be, on the limitations of our own attitudes, beliefs and expectations.

All such relationships have a high risk of becoming unhappy—toxic even—very quickly. And toxicity brings unhappiness and distress.

The causes of such problems need to be examined carefully and resolved, before the relationship becomes irretrievably damaged.

Why and how does this happen? What are the circumstances that create the imbalance? Why is this more likely between some individuals than others?

There are multiple reasons and we will explore several of them in order to provide guidance and advice on how to address each issue, learn important new skills and thus substantially increase the chances of a successful and happy outcome.

The first thing to examine is what happens in the mind when individuals first meet. We can then discover why people react the way they do based on their own personality preferences, what to do to manage this process and how to unblock potential problems.

This will provide the key to establishing successful relationships with anyone.

Establishing rapport

When strangers meet each other for the first time, especially in unfamiliar locations or situations, there is a very rapid first reaction from a most primitive part of the brain, the amygdala, which is responsible for heightening our awareness of danger and perception of fear, anger, sadness and aggression, preparing the body to fight or flee.

This is a natural defence mechanism, which was most valuable at a time when life was hazardous and split-second decisions were required for survival. Decisions had to be made quickly. Friend or foe? Do I need to run away fast, or get ready to fight?

In most of the situations we experience today, which are generally much less threatening, these reactions, whilst still present, are much more subdued.

They can express themselves, though, in such forms as mild aggression, excessive or overly hard handshaking, looking away, and sullenness or even (especially in the case of angst-ridden teenagers) a refusal to say hello altogether.

Once these preliminaries are over, the subconscious mind takes over and decides what attitude to take to the stranger. How does it do this?

The subconscious mind has stored the details of all previous encounters and selects the ones that most fit the current situation. It has stored how people looked, dressed, behaved and acted, how loud or quiet they were, how fascinating or boring they appeared to be and makes a judgment based on this mass of historical data, however inaccurate it may be.

It uses this information primarily to protect its host. The subconscious mind is in fact **looking for itself**. It is looking for **someone like me**, its **mirror image**, because someone like me is likely to be the best and safest option.

When strangers assemble for the first time, it can be observed how, fairly rapidly, they form into groups.

These groups will appear, at least on the surface, to be very homogeneous and the homogeneity will be in terms of participants' age, gender, appearance, clothing, hairstyle, facial expression and/or social background.

The whole process is entirely subconscious. The subconscious mind of each participant is making judgments on 'who is most like me' and naturally gravitating towards them.

As the participants start to know and understand each other better, the groupings will change quite naturally as the subconscious mind makes adjustments based on new data and updated assessments on who is 'most like me'.

But what does 'most like me' mean? What are the elements that the subconscious mind is looking for as it makes its assessments?

This needs careful examination in order to be able to manage and develop meaningful, satisfying and beneficial relationships **even when two people are not like each other.**

Establishing just such relationships is important, valuable and enriching precisely because it enables a wider perspective to be taken, new knowledge and understanding to be gleaned and wisdom to be acquired from sources not usually tapped. Why deprive yourself of such an opportunity just because someone appears to be different?

Numerous psychographic studies have been conducted on this topic over many years, but there is much still to discover and learn.

Here is one analysis of the six areas that have the most significant impact on relationships and on understanding what 'most like me' means.

The six areas are: energy and drive; the way information is viewed and assimilated; the way

decisions are taken; lifestyle management; empathy, warmth and sincerity; and a sense of humour.

Energy and drive

People's energy and drive can be anywhere on a line between high and low.

High energy, high drive people, who are often referred to as 'extroverts', will naturally gravitate to likeminded souls and will be happy talking and exchanging views at length and sometimes quite noisily over long periods of time.

They **gain more energy** from these exchanges and will seem to have a substantial capacity for socializing. They are happy to get on their soap box and may be difficult to stop. Their energy comes from and is increased by the exchanges they have with other people.

On the other hand, low energy, low drive people, often referred to as 'introverts', derive their energy from 'me time', when they can relax and recover on their own, because they become exhausted rather than exhilarated by exchanges with other people.

They can perform perfectly well during such interactions, but they will need to recharge their energy batteries sooner and more frequently. They need their **quiet time**.

These two types are very different and have very **different needs**.

When they come together, the differences they have on this dimension creates an obvious potential for discord. While one is getting more and more animated, the other is getting more and more tired, so that the possibility of misunderstanding becomes greater: one risks being seen as brash and loud, the other as dull and boring.

With skilful management, however, these differences can be understood and overcome in the longer term.

To start with, the differences need to be acknowledged and respected, with a full exposure of why and how these differences are occurring. This is followed either by an open discussion on what actions to take to mitigate the problem or, with experience, a personal reflection on what is happening and appropriate adjustment made to **one's own behaviour.**

If we want to change how the exchange goes and the perception one is creating, the change has to be from the inside of oneself first. Any attempt to change anyone else is wrong and arrogant and will fail.

Only then can solutions be found to accommodate the differences and turn a potentially difficult relationship into a positive one.

Consider this case. A married couple were both lecturers and professors in the same subject on the same, well-attended and acclaimed management courses. Both were highly regarded by the faculty and by students.

The wife was high energy, high drive, and 'extroverted', the husband low energy, low drive and more 'introverted'. When they conducted their courses, they would perform very professionally and achieved consistently high rates for their lectures and the management of their courses.

The issues, however, would surface in the post-lecture period.

The high energy, high drive lecturer was happy to mingle with the students till late in the evening and considered it part of her role, while the low energy, low drive lecturer needed his quiet time and would slip away early to recuperate.

This was starting to create serious problems in their relationship.

The high energy, high drive lecturer felt that she was shouldering the greater part of the workload and was contributing much more to supporting the students after work.

The low energy, low drive lecturer felt unappreciated for his highly competent lecturing skills, careful reflections on the course content and ongoing adjustments to it. He also felt somewhat demotivated and tired.

The relationship was becoming asymmetrical.

It was at this point that they sought help.

This was the solution:

1. To ensure that both parties understood fully what the differences in energy levels were and how each had differing needs for recuperation. It was not that the low energy lecturer was unable to mingle or that he did not wish to do so, it was simply that he needed to create quiet time during which he could recharge his batteries, if he was to undertake this task with the enthusiasm it warranted.

   Similarly, the high energy lecturer needed to understand that her highly intense post lecture activities were not necessarily always welcomed by the students, who also had their differing energy needs, as well as the requirement to study. She also needed to appreciate the important work being done by her husband on the course content in between sessions and that reflecting on the course content and making adjustments based on these reflections was a shared responsibility.

2. To adjust the work and lecture schedule (and build in reflection time) to create space for recuperation and thus enable the low energy, low drive lecturer to participate in post-lecture activities.

   They also agreed that, after a period of post-lecture activity, they would both leave at the same time, showing alignment and harmony on the part of the lecturers and allowing time for the students to complete their assignments.

The solution was therefore based on an open discussion of what was happening in the mind of the two lecturers, why they felt the way they did, a proper understanding of the differences that existed and then a creative and sympathetic give-and-take approach to its resolution.

The way information is viewed and assimilated.

People absorb information and manage it in very different ways.

In order to make sense of the information received, some will look for big pictures, exciting patterns and connections while others will look for detail and logical understanding.

The first group will be more interested in creative aspects while the other will be more interested in analytical aspects.

The creative group will use more of the right side of the brain to stimulate their imagination, developing ideas, concepts and images of what the possibilities might be. They will create opportunities from the information received and enjoy the visions they have created—even if they are sometimes rather optimistic!

The analytical group, unimpressed by the flights of fancy and woolly 'blue sky thinking' of the creative group, will take a calm, serious, sceptical approach and ensure in their own minds that the information they have received adds up, makes sense and is logically correct. Until they reach that point, they will feel distinctly uncomfortable. The certainty they need is missing.

Many a project or plan has failed miserably because the creative group's enthusiasm was not tempered by the analytical group's wise common sense. And the schemes that they dreamt up were sometimes much more expensive, a source of friction and disharmony and ultimately unworkable.

There **was** someone in the group, which consisted mainly of creative types, with an appropriately analytical mind, who could have helped. Carried by their enthusiastic reverie, none of the 'creatives' thought to ask him their opinion. They would most likely have been considered spoilsports and boring and ignored anyway.

Similarly, many brilliant projects have been abandoned because the analytical types, who represented the majority, could not get 'the numbers to add up' and never gained the certainty they craved. Had they asked the creative type whether some changes could be made to improve the financials and reduce the uncertainty and risk, they could have transformed the project into a significant success. But they didn't trust the creative person sufficiently to ask.

As individuals, couples or groups we need both types of thinking in our lives.

We need to have access to creativity and imaginative thinking as well as an understanding of detail and workability. One without the other is always going to run the risk of being sub-optimal.

Understanding this fact and actively seeking both is essential to mental development and growth as well as excellent relationships.

While the differences in the way information is processed will tend to divide the two types, seeking out those with different approaches is extremely important, to avoid costly mistakes and also to stimulate and stretch the mind, find innovative solutions and learn.

The way decisions are taken

The continuum here is between decision-making based predominantly on emotions and decision-making based on results.

The group who are emotion based will take decisions when they **feel comfortable** with it. If others are involved in the decision, they will delay until such time as they **feel that everybody is comfortable**.

Until then, they will question and probe, suggest alternatives, try different approaches, even abandon the decision altogether or at the very least delay it. Time is less important than alignment.

A potential pitfall at this stage is that 'analysis paralysis' occurs. No decision is taken because there never is enough information with which to be comfortable enough to take one. And there never will be! Complete certainty does not exist and there is always risk in any decision.

What is often forgotten, however, is that sometimes the greatest risk lies in doing nothing, postponing, asking for more studies, doing more research, anything to avoid making a decision. This then becomes a fear of getting it wrong and ultimately being blamed or blaming oneself (a vestige of past parental expectations).

No decisions can be based on perfect information or perfect alignment or hundred percent certainty. Life is not like that. Allowing this to become a wonderful excuse for indecision and to waste time on seeking alignment with others **or alignment with one's own mind** is a recipe for anxiety and unhappiness. It reduces one's inner strength.

Another risk of this group is that the search for alignment leads to a sub-standard result, especially if the people who are part of the process are all predominantly emotion-driven decision takers. They may opt for the solution that they can all feel comfortable with but which is itself the worst one and a poor compromise. *They have preferred alignment to action.*

The group who have preference to action, on the other hand, will take decisions based on **achieving a result**, preferably in the most efficient and timely manner possible. The problem is that, in their mind, if others don't like it, it's just too bad! This is a recipe for resentment and rejection.

To this group, alignment is less important than efficiency and time management. *Urgency requires quick decisions. Taking time to get everyone on board is a luxury that they believe doesn't exist.*

The obvious risk here is that decisions are made quickly and arbitrarily without considering their full effect, especially on other people. No time is devoted to ensuring there is a 'buy-in' either in one's own mind or by colleagues. We are all human beings who act based on how we feel rather than what we may logically believe.

> *When dealing with people remember you are not dealing with creatures of logic, but creatures of emotion.*

Taking decisions that affect others without due consideration for their feelings or the impact this will have on them is a recipe for discord and disharmony.

If people feel ignored or bullied, they will be hurt and resentful and, as in physics, there will be an equal and opposite reaction. This resentment has been known to lead to actions to sabotage the plan.

Obviously this can be the cause of considerable stress when the two extremes meet.

One wants to be sure all options have been examined and everyone is happy with the decision, while the other simply wants to get it done.

Here again, there are no right or wrongs. It all depends on the circumstances.

If alignment is important—for example, when several people are involved or when the individual is unsure on which course to take and needs to consult widely before making a decision—then basing the decision on the emotions being satisfied is perfectly sensible.

Similarly, when time is short and decisions are needed, then achieving a decision efficiently and quickly is also perfectly sensible and pragmatic. You don't need to get everybody aligned if the house is on fire!

Dealing with this is, once again, based on understanding the situation realistically first.

Is alignment of all the participants really that critical? Will the decision-makers or participants be happy with a majority point of view? Is it really necessary to take that decision right now rather than 'sleep on it'? Would a few more searches, or enquiries or another study not be worth waiting for?

Understanding the situation and the underlying needs and wants of each person involved and the extent to which they can contribute to the decision is also important. Do they have knowledge vital to the decision or is their need really to be acknowledged or just to be asked?

Knowing and reflecting on these underlying issues will often enable a wiser decision to be taken, perhaps even quicker and without running roughshod over the emotions of the participants.

Lifestyle management

Some people are naturally more relaxed about their lives, while others have higher stress levels. Some are happy to 'go with the flow' while others have a greater need to plan and organize. Differences in life management can be the source of significant anxiety and disharmony.

Take the case of a couple, one of whom is fairly laid-back (and 'last minute', another characteristic of this type) and the other is more about being organized, when deciding on their next holiday.

The organized one starts planning a year in advance in order to get the best deal in the right location and wants certainty. The idea of leaving it to the last minute and risking not getting a flight is abhorrent.

When the organized one asks the more laid-back one, in June, **a year before** she has in mind to fix the holiday, where he would like to go on his holiday, he gives his reply on **his** time horizon, which is **this weekend.** The idea of trying to plan that much ahead is simply incomprehensible to the laid-back person and he considers his partner to be ridiculously over-organized, verging on 'OCD'.

Getting them to agree to discuss a holiday, let alone arrive at an agreement will take some effort to avoid both getting stressed for very different reasons.

Take the case of the executive with a more relaxed approach who is asked to prepare a report for Monday, the following week, this being Wednesday. She accepts the assignment and they agree delivery for Monday morning at 9.00 am.

She thinks about the assignment in her head, realizes she will need quiet thinking time and decides she will complete it on Sunday afternoon.

Her boss, the organized one, walks past her office on several occasions that same Wednesday and asks her how she is getting on. She says, fine. Seeing no evidence of physical progress, he gets increasingly stressed. He cannot stop himself from regularly checking and gets more and more agitated.

Eventually, he goes in to see her and, now very stressed, asks her why she hasn't started, whether she intends to do the project after all or whether he should find someone else to complete it. She is surprised and hurt and wonders whether he believes her capable of undertaking the assignment. She says, with some barely concealed anger, that it will be ready on Monday morning *as agreed*.

And it is and is perfectly done.

The issue is not one of competence but life style expectation. They have different life management needs and preferences, which affect how they see the world.

It is, as before, not about right and wrong. **It is all about understanding the other person and making appropriate *changes to one's own perception.***

Clearly if there had been a question of incompetence or laziness, the situation would have required different handling. But it was purely a question of life management and 'we all get to Christmas at the same time!'

Under such circumstances there is no value whatever in trying to change someone else's preferences, even if that were possible. What is more important is to understand the differences, build new skills and adjust one's own behaviour accordingly.

The secret of change is to focus your energy,
not on fighting the old, but on building the new.
Dan Millman

Empathy, warmth and sincerity

The first four psychological characteristics have been on a continuum from one extreme to the other where none are either good or bad. They are simply preferences. The important factor is to understand the preference differences between individuals, what happens when they interact and how to manage them effectively.

The next two characteristics—empathy, warmth and sincerity and a sense of humour—are different in that low is less good than high.

Having high levels will increase the ability to establish good relationships, while having low levels will limit this capacity. It is therefore beneficial to understand how to improve and then learn and exercise in order to become more successful.

Empathy is the ability and desire to understand and share another person's feelings from their perspective, to place oneself in their shoes and experience emotionally what they are experiencing. *Compassion* and *sympathy* are closely linked to empathy, and are feelings of care for someone in need and the desire to help them.

Studies have shown clearly that empathy and a higher EQ (emotional quotient) encourage the development of positive social relationships, the ability to relate to others, to establish effective rapport and to mediate.

Children (and adults) can and should be helped and encouraged to learn to become more empathetic.

This can be done by having them imagine themselves in the shoes of others (whether real cases or from stories) and learning to understand and identify their own feelings.

Doing this subtly but regularly will help the child develop her sensitivity to others and enhance her care and consideration for others.

Empathy is usually separated into **cognitive empathy**—the ability to understand another's perspective or mental condition (but not necessarily agree with it)—and **affective or emotional empathy**—the ability to be affected by another's emotional state and to respond appropriately.

Empathy is a skill that is, to a certain degree, innate, but which can also be learnt and nurtured. Empathy gradually develops through life and is greatly enhanced by having experienced similar difficult situations, which increases greater empathic understanding.

Warmth—a sincere understanding and caring for others—invites and inspires trust, while *sincerity* creates a spontaneously authentic and truthful environment.

Studies have shown that the best outcomes of counselling are not nearly as much to do with the technical skills of the counsellor as they are of his/her emotional level of warmth, empathy and sincerity aligned with understanding and directly relevant experience.

This indicates the extent to which these abilities are vital to establish rapport and create positive relationships.

The higher the level of empathy, warmth and sincerity, the greater the ability to establish effective and fruitful relationships.

What are the best ways to demonstrate these every day?

1. Listen and pay attention.

2. Make and hold eye contact.

3. Find commonalities.

4. Smile, especially when the other person smiles.

5. Be authentic, polite, supportive, uplifting, enthusiastic and kind.

6. Take responsibility for actions.

7. Be prepared to be vulnerable.

8. Trust, in order to be trusted.

9. Do not blame others.

Most of these are very obvious, but surprisingly difficult to do well, consistently and in differing or difficult situations.

This is particularly the case in the high-speed, stressed and rushed environment in which we live. An environment that encourages selfishness over altruism ('I have no time to listen or help') and restricts the time available for what many may see as niceties but which are essentials to relationship building and obtaining positive results.

Listening and paying attention

This list of possible actions to demonstrate empathy are largely self-explanatory.

Let us consider two very important ones in more detail:

1. Listening and paying attention
2. Establishing trust

Listening and paying attention are much harder than usually imagined and yet in many respects are the most important of all.

> *We have two ears and one mouth so that*
> *we can listen twice as much as we speak.*
> **An old proverb**

Sometimes we have so much we would like to transmit and we are so keen to get it all out in time lest we forget what we were going to say, that we fail to turn the receiver on.

This is especially so for the high energy-high drive group and the results-based decision taker.

There are three main ways to listen:

1. Listening to learn

2. Listening to evaluate

3. Listening openly.

1. Listening to learn

Listening to learn happens in most daily activities, such as listening to the news or advice. A certain amount of concentration is required as well as some conscious effort—especially to quieten down our self-talk, which will try to interfere with our thinking process and disturb our concentration.

This mode of listening is often associated with taking notes so as to be able to review the information later on.

When establishing or developing relationships, however, this type of listening is insufficient because the act of taking notes detracts from being able to **listen completely.** If you are writing, you cannot be listening at the same time.

2. Listening to evaluate

Listening to evaluate, also known as critical listening requires more concentration and effort than listening to learn, and is about making judgments and analysing detail.

This entails an active engagement of the brain to decipher what is being said and to make assessments, such as: 'I like what I'm hearing.' 'This is very different from my own beliefs.' 'Why would the speaker think that?' 'Where did that opinion come from?'

Listening to evaluate is a very important way of learning as it requires the brain to take in information, compare it with other data previously stored and then make decisions and judgments.

It runs the risk, however, that we substitute our own opinions and biases for those of the person we are listening to.

The efficiency of the learning process is impaired, especially if, at the same time, our self-talk is working overtime interjecting pre-judgements or prejudices.

We cannot listen well if we think we already know.

It is impossible for a person to begin to learn what he thinks he already knows.
Epictetus

3. Listening openly

The third way of listening, and the one that is most appropriate for establishing and building relationships, is to listen openly, also known as empathic or active listening.

Listening openly means focusing one's entire being on what the other person is saying, without interruption, without judgment, without trying to find solutions, without allowing that inner voice to interfere and without giving advice.

The only objective is to understand properly what is being said and the emotions that lie behind it. **It is listening with the innocence of the child and not the conviction of the adult.** Nothing else gets in the way.

When someone listens openly, their eyes open more widely (to absorb more information) and focus more intently on the speaker.

They are taking in the information with their ears but also with their eyes and other senses in order to receive the greatest amount of data and interpret not only the words used, but often more importantly, nonverbal cues such as body language, facial expression, breathing, tone of voice and eye movement.

After the speaker has finished, the active, open listener may paraphrase what has been said, not with a view to agreeing or disagreeing (which would signify making a judgment) but to check that they have understood properly what is being said, to avoid misunderstanding and build trust.

If the listener paraphrases well, they have obviously been listening and an atmosphere of cooperation can start to be created.

Building trust

Trust has to be earned. It is not a right. It cannot be assumed. It cannot be requested. It takes time, patience, understanding and respect. It develops over time and becomes something very special shared between individuals. It is a fundamental building block of real friendship and happiness. It is a major key to establishing and keeping good relationships.

It can, however, be easily and quickly destroyed.

If you want to be trusted, be trustworthy. This means worthy of someone's trust.

How is trust built and how does one become worthy of another's trust?

Plato believed that in order to achieve happiness, human beings must be consciously moral and develop wisdom, courage, moderation and justice.

Aristotle believed that this required not just reflection but also action. It needed to be practised every day.

Wisdom and justice encompass and depend on trust.

Trustworthy people have the following characteristics.

1. They are honest. They do not lie, steal or mislead. They are straightforward, do not manipulate or seek to control.

2. They have integrity and respect for all people, whatever their background, belief, colour or creed.

3. They are loyal to friends and family. They help and support them unselfishly in times of need. They cherish and nurture them in their growth and praise them in their successes. They defend them against gossip and negative talk.

4. Their word is their bond. When they make a promise, they keep it.

5. They are dependable. When they undertake a task, they deliver and can be relied on to do the right thing.

6. They keep the confidences and secrets that others entrust to them.

7. They are gentle with other's feelings.

8. They are not afraid to say they are wrong or that they do not know. They are not afraid of change.

9. They seek the truth and inspire confidence.

If someone is able to convince me and show me that what I do or think is not right, I will gladly change; for I seek the truth, by which no one was ever injured.
Marcus Aurelius

A sense of humour

Humour is a wonderful stress reliever. It lightens the atmosphere and defuses potentially tense situations. Laughter is a great healer and rejuvenates the soul.

It requires subtlety, sensitivity, good listening and observation skills, a way with words and courage. It should only be used in the right situation and with the right audience—to not cause offence.

Having a sense of humour helps establish and maintain good relationships, but only if done well.

This is not about the ability to tell jokes and it is absolutely not about doing so at others' expense. It is about finding what is amusing in a situation, however silly, and laughing at it together so that the experience is uplifting for all.

People who can laugh at themselves become more vulnerable to others, which increases their own humanity and attractiveness. They show that they do not take themselves too seriously and are thus more likely to be better companions.

This also builds their resilience because, when problems occur, they can see the lighter side, have a better perspective and are better able to let go of negative feelings and move on.

I've also regarded a sense of humour as one of the most important things on a big expedition. When you're in a difficult or dangerous situation, or when you're depressed about the chances of success, someone who can make you laugh eases the tension.
Edmund Hillary

Laughing at the same jokes or the same situations also creates a connection with another person and a common bond, helping to build a stronger, more intimate relationship.

Imagination was given to a man to compensate him for what he is not. A sense of humour to console him for what he is.

Having a sense of humour requires creativity in finding the right words to deliver a clever witticism, an amusing repartee or a juxtaposed, surprising image.

It means having the ability to see that much of life is absurd and random and to draw comic inferences and incongruous images whose surreal quality amuse by their very absurdity. Spontaneous creativity creates ideas that delight.

Sometimes the simplest situations can amuse, but it is only the people with a sense of humour who will laugh.

In order to develop a sense of humour, watch humourous programmes, listen to amusing podcasts, look for cartoons in the papers, read funny books and go to comedies at the theatre.

By immersing oneself in humour, humour becomes part of the soul. This cannot help but enhance one's sense of humour.

A sense of humour, once developed, is forever.

You don't stop laughing when you grow old,
you grow old when you stop laughing.

Mirroring

Having now examined some characteristics or traits of what 'looks like me' might mean for our subconscious mind, it is clear that this is a very complex subject, easily prone to misinterpretation and error, which is why so many relationships are, at best, lukewarm.

When people who have very different preferences and characteristics meet up, the likelihood of disharmony will be very high as they will see themselves as coming from different planets.

The subconscious mind of the individuals concerned, while seeking to find its mirror image, will most likely not have the skills to adjust well to the differences encountered and the exchange ends up in discord and creates an unsatisfactory relationship.

One often hears the phrase 'I keep making the same mistake,' and this is in significant part because the person has not been exposed to or learnt the

subtleties of the different characteristics described—
let alone how to manage them.

They may think, again and again, that they have
found the perfect friend, colleague or partner, only to
realize subsequently the huge differences that exist between them. They were not looking with the right eyes
at the right things.

Another common phrase is 'opposites attract'.
The reality is very different. People may think they
are attracted to their 'opposite' when, in reality, on the
six characteristics described above, their deep attach-
ment is to people similar to themselves. They have not
understood what the important elements are and why
what they consider to be 'differences' are actually only
variations of the same trait.

With our newfound knowledge of some of these
traits, let us now examine the concept and power of
'mirroring'.

People will be more trustful of those with whom
they feel a natural affinity and less trustful of those
who seem different. This is the basis of all human
prejudice.

In order to have the best possible chance of establishing a relationship of trust with another person who
seems, on the surface, to be different, we need not to

try to change them but to change ourselves to be more like them.

Mirroring means observing the other person's body language, tone of voice, speed of speech, breathing, language and words used and beliefs and then adjusting our own behaviour to more closely match that of the other person.

This has to be done sensitively and subtly.

The objective, and the only objective, is to establish a good relationship with someone else **by making efforts to see, feel and interpret the world through their eyes and thus create a connection.**

If this sounds like gross manipulation it isn't— for several reasons.

People see through manipulation very quickly and if the approach is not authentic the attempt at mirroring will fail.

Genuine mirroring requires paying close attention and listening carefully to what the other person is saying and feeling. This cannot be done well if the one mirroring is self-absorbed or has an ulterior motive.

Mirroring cannot be faked and the surprising thing is that, while the person being mirrored may start off as a stranger, the act of mirroring will make them seem 'more like me' to my subconscious mind *as I continue to alter my own behaviour.*

The very act of listening actively and observing carefully is a welcome signal of consideration.

Matching body posture, intensity and rhythm of speech, use of words and philosophical beliefs (unless they are objectionable for any reason) creates a state of agreement with the other person and the other person's subconscious will respond positively to the attention shown.

An understanding of neuro-linguistic programming (NLP) is of help here. The words used and the feelings demonstrated by a person are strong indicators of that person's 'code', of how they subjectively and consciously experience the world and the verbal and non-verbal communication patterns they use to do so.

If a person experiences the world primarily through visual images, they will use words which have visual connotations, such as, 'Do you *see* what I mean?' and create vivid images.

If they are more attuned to receiving their signals about the world through sound, they will use words with auditory connotations, 'How does that *sound* to you?'

If they are primarily kinaesthetic in their subjective subconscious experience, they will use words of feeling and tactile sensations, 'How do you *feel* about that?'

A person whose code is VAK (visual, auditory, kinaesthetic, in that order) will enjoy using imaginative language and images but will most likely not like touching.

A person whose code is AKV will respond best to soft melodious tones and voices, not strident ones, and will be less impressed with grand imaginative tableaus.

A person whose code is KVA will like to feel, sense and touch but may not be so good at listening.

Of course this is a gross oversimplification, but it does provide another insight into how people view the world and another tool by which to achieve successful mirroring.

In the same way as we examined the potential issues that result from people's differing energy, thought processes, decision-making and lifestyle needs, so too, we need to assess the issues that result from their differing NLP characteristics.

If people with very different NLP profiles want to establish good relationships, they will need to be aware of and adjust to these differences.

For example, a primarily kinaesthetic person will respond best to words and behaviours that appeal to the senses. They will enjoy physical closeness, holding hands, touching and feeling. They *need* to feel and touch their universe.

If their partner has a low kinaesthetic sense, they will find this uncomfortable, as if something is missing, as if they are unable to show their true caring and loving self. They will view their partner as somewhat cold and unreceptive. To them feeling and touching are prime signals of warmth and togetherness.

On the other hand, a primarily visual person with a low kinaesthetic sense will be uncomfortable with touching or holding hands, preferring visual clues such as being well groomed, properly turned out, clean and attractive to the eye.

In order to find happiness, they will need to discuss openly their differing needs and reactions and learn how to develop all their senses. If they are to be happy together, they will want to learn how all their senses can be nurtured to please their partner. This will not only make them open to new sensations but also create positive energy and enhance inner well-being.

Mirroring enables people to understand more effectively what motivates and stimulates others and thus serves to establish good relationships with almost anyone.

This is an enriching and happy experience and the basis for widening one's circle of friends, as well as learning more broadly and more completely.

Letting go

In creating, maintaining and nurturing excellent relationships (as well as living a less stressful life) it is important to recognize the importance of being able to 'let go'.

Letting go, a key Stoic philosophy, means we acknowledge our limitations when it comes to our relationships and that we cannot change things we cannot control or seek to change people.

If we try to do this, we will only inevitably become frustrated and angry and may in fact promote the opposite of what we are seeking to achieve. We also reduce our self-esteem.

Any person capable of angering you becomes your master; he can anger you only when you permit yourself to be disturbed by him.

For example, when we are communicating with a colleague by text or email, and are in a hurry, if we do not receive a quick reply, how do we react? How do we interpret the lack of response? And what do we then do?

Unless we are able to let go—because we cannot control the response—we will quite probably start to think 'something's not right.' Maybe the other party is ignoring us. Maybe they no longer wish to talk to us. Maybe they are not well. Maybe, maybe, maybe. Before long we start imagining the worst.

And yet, in the vast majority of instances, there is a simple and innocent reason for the delay. The other person had just jumped into a car to go to their next appointment. Their next meeting had just started and they were unable to respond immediately. They had other more urgent messages to deal with. They had to go and pick up the children.

We attribute, quite unnecessarily, motives and feelings to what were purely imagined occurrences. Our inherent fears, stimulated by our subconscious mind and previous experience, overwhelm our sense of reality.

> *We suffer more often in*
> *imagination than in reality.*
> **Seneca**

If we had simply let go, because we cannot (and should not) control the actions of another, then we would have avoided the frustration, stress and even anger caused by our perception of the situation.

And if we had continued to bombard them with more texts, we would have risked angering them and worsening the problem—all quite unnecessarily.

If you are distressed by anything external,
the pain is not due to the thing itself,
but rather to your estimate of it; and this
you have the power to revoke at any moment.
Marcus Aurelius

If we want our relationships to thrive, we need to learn to let go by saying to ourselves that anything we cannot control is okay and we'll move on.

Once we have decided to let go, because it's okay, our insecurities diminish to the point of non-existence. What could have resulted in a serious misunderstanding and a damaged relationship has been avoided.

We have to develop the inner power to decide to let go and thus eliminate the control that outside events would otherwise have on us.

You have power over your mind—not outside
events. Realize this and you will find strength.

However close a relationship with another, we should always acknowledge, respect and celebrate the fact that there are two separate people with separate identities, needs and wants.

Some people, for various psychological reasons usually acquired in childhood, have greater need for, say, reassurance, praise, certainty, control or perfection. They, most of all, need to learn to let go, because they are most at risk of displaying the stressed reactions that can be so disruptive.

This is where letting go is vital but also most difficult.

Problems will arise if their needs swamp the one who does not have such requirements. If they need to be constantly in charge or have everything just right or be frequently recognized even for relatively trivial matters, it will overwhelm the other, and the relationship will inevitably falter.

This is especially so if accompanied by a desire to know everything all the time—another expression of control, which leads to constant and stressful questioning both of self and the other.

In many ways, letting go is an effective form of anti-stress therapy because, practised regularly, it enables the mind to avoid negative emotional responses such as anxiety and anger and helps develop and nurture strong and lasting relationships.

Letting go also protects in times of real difficulties because it instills a sense of acceptance, and a calmer call to action, while avoiding the trauma of a single major aspiration, ambition or relationship going wrong.

It is sometimes also useful to remember that we are on this earth for a very short time and the little things that frustrate and annoy us are really of no significance compared to the enormous injustices that exist in the world.

We should live each day as if it is our last. We should thus think, do and be good while we can. All our relationships will benefit from this.

We must be willing to get rid of the life we've planned, so as to have the life that is waiting for us.
Joseph Campbell

Letting go all else, cling to the following few truths. Remember that man lives only in the present, in this fleeting instant: all the rest of his life is either past and gone, or not yet revealed. This mortal life is a little thing, lived in a little corner of the earth: and little too is the longest fame to come, dependent as it is on a succession

of fast-perishing little men who have
no knowledge even of their own selves,
much less of one long dead and gone.
Marcus Aurelius

Love

This section on the happiness of relationships would not be complete without a final word on the overwhelming importance of love.

Amor vincit omnia—Love conquers all.

All the advice provided in this section is to help to create the circumstances in which happy relationships can be created, unhappy relationships corrected and love can flourish.

Love is a deep feeling of affection of one person for another. It is always personal and individual.

When people talk of loving a group of people or a family, they mean loving each individual person separately as a unique and complete human being.

The absence of a loved one compresses the heart and it aches. Expecting the return of a loved one creates longing and the warm glow of expectation. Being with a loved one eliminates the concept of time, as it ceases to exist.

Romantic love is also about passion and sexual desire and these strong emotional feelings are wonderful and perfectly normal and truly beneficial expressions of mutual enjoyment and happiness.

Romantic love alone, however blissful, is not enough to sustain a loving relationship over time. Love has to be nurtured by much deeper, subtler, more complex and longer-lasting expressions of devotion.

Love, which is encompassed by all the guidance provided so far, is about:

1. unconditional affection, understanding and acceptance

2. responsibility, patience and letting go any ideas of control

3. unselfish devotion and dedication

4. confidence and dependence

5. gentleness, kindness and warmth

6. wanting rather than needing

7. giving and receiving

8. nurturing and protecting

*Love hinders death. Love is life. ... Love is God,
and to die means that I, a particle of love, shall
return to the general and eternal source.*
Leo Tolstoy

*Love is patient, love is kind. It does not envy,
it does not boast, it is not proud. It is not rude,
it is not self-seeking. It is not easily angered; it
keeps no record of wrongs. Love does not delight
in evil, but rejoices with the truth. It always
protects, always trusts, always hopes, and
always perseveres. Love never fails.*
1 Corinthians 13:4–8

*In the end these things matter most:
How well did you love? How fully did you live?
How deeply did you let go?*
Jack Kornfield writing about Buddhist ideas

*Love is the energizing elixir of the universe,
the cause and effect of all harmonies.*
Anon

It should now be evident that we have arrived at
the last step, the happiness of harmony.

THE FIFTH STEP:

THE HAPPINESS OF HARMONY

The fifth step, the happiness of harmony, comprises the best of all the previous steps: the intense feelings of happiness when achieving something difficult; the joy of helping another and giving of oneself; and the deeply personal and warm, intimate sense of affection and love from personal relationships.

The results of an extensive international study showed a clear cross-cultural trend for considering happiness in terms of inner peace and harmony, with two powerful contextual factors. The first was associated with good relationships and the second with physical health.

Good relationships satisfy a critical psychosocial need to be known and valued, and this comes from having excellent relationships with family, friends and the communities in which we live. But is this enough for inner peace and the harmony of the soul?

174

True inner peace and harmony is much more complex, much more difficult to achieve and requires a much deeper examination and understanding.

Before we can achieve true inner peace and harmony we need to be able to perceive, with total clarity and honesty, the good and the bad around us and appreciate how we react to it, as well as the good and the bad in ourselves and how we manage, address or ignore that.

The happiness of harmony cannot exist if we choose to block out or conveniently ignore what is around us or inside us.

How often do we choose to ignore the suffering that we experience around us or the disharmony that we experience internally when things don't go our way, when we are angry, anxious, frustrated, stressed or just sad? We simply allow these emotions to flood us without any consideration as to their real cause or effect. We do not take the time to examine properly the cause of our disquiet, what has given rise to it, whether it is justified or what lessons we might learn.

Buddhist teaching recognizes that the causes of disquiet need to be considered carefully and that life entails external and internal suffering. This is part of the human condition. To be alive is to experience suffering—at least at times. Without suffering there is no true understanding of life or a capacity to experience its opposite, joy.

Attempts to block out, ignore or banish suffering from the mind will ultimately fail and cause further disharmony of the soul.

Blocking out suffering is known to create mental disorders, such as those experienced by people who have suffered severe trauma, if they are unable to face, let alone process, their experiences.

Buddhism teaches us not to try to run away from suffering. You have to confront suffering. You have to look deeply into the nature of suffering in order to recognize its cause, the making of the suffering.
Thich Nhat Hanh

To achieve the happiness of harmony, we have to come to terms with the inescapable fact that life is not just about joy but also about suffering. We then have to learn to accept and manage this fundamental truth. We have to learn to understand our own consciousness and develop compassion as part of our quest for inner peace. Compassion enables us to handle suffering.

To develop our own consciousness in a way that can foster inner peace and mental harmony, we have to learn to be true to ourselves. We have to consciously and deliberately do our best to learn wisdom, compassion and justice, while helping to protect, heal and bring peace to our world in whatever ways we are able. This has to be our prime motivation and intention.

To gain true happiness the mind has to transcend to a new and higher level of understanding in which we begin to discover our inner soul and combine all our many senses to perceive everything that surrounds us. Only by being conscious of what we truly feel and understanding the source of these feelings in order to make better choices on how we live, can we understand what our soul is and what our role and purpose should be.

You don't have a soul.
You ARE a soul.
You have a body.

This will gradually emerge from a proper awareness of all those feelings associated with each element of happiness and unhappiness that is experienced, together with an acceptance of life as it truly and honestly is, and of oneself as a mortal, humble and fallible human being trying nevertheless to do the best he or she can.

Happiness is when what you think,
what you say, and what you do are in harmony.
Vedic injunction

Awareness

Developing an acute awareness of both the external world and our own internal mind and thoughts is essential.

The external world includes everything that we experience as an outsider looking in. This includes all of the environment in which we live and that we observe; the seas, the mountains and valleys, the streams, the flowers, art, music, sculpture, poetry, prose, architecture, science and so on.

It also includes all those things that we observe unhappily; suffering, poverty, sickness, cruelty, neglect and anguish of all kinds, for which we need to develop a real sense of compassion and justice, not just a passing and short-lived reflection to assuage feelings of guilt.

Have compassion for all beings,
rich and poor alike; each has their suffering.

Developing a heightened awareness of our external world and inner mind is not at all easy. But that doesn't mean we shouldn't make the effort to keep trying and learning. Because herein lies the secret of inner harmony and peace.

We need to develop our ability to appreciate the moment in which we find ourselves, without concerns about the past or fears about the future; just focusing on the present moment.

> *Do not dwell in the past,*
> *do not dream of the future, concentrate*
> *the mind on the present moment.*
> **Buddhist sutra**

By learning to focus on the present moment, we gradually, over time, develop a better appreciation of everything that surrounds us; of our friends, our family, our communities, our world and our universe, right down to all the small but nevertheless significant elements that animate, enrich and gladden our lives.

As we learn to appreciate more profoundly, with all our senses, what is all around us and what our true inner thoughts are, so we also start to develop a greater depth of feeling and understanding of who we are and why we exist.

Too often, we are too busy in our daily lives to become consciously aware of what is going on around us and we miss out on the many opportunities for learning, reflecting, understanding and happiness.

Being increasingly aware of what is going on inside our own mind, our true self, requires courage and honesty.

We need to be mindful that we have a number of selves.

There is the 'present' self that experiences the world, that is curious about its environment and that learns and absorbs. This is the first-person experience that is present during the waking day and can learn to be in the moment. It is where memories are first built and it is these memories that serve to fill out our personality.

Throughout life we lay down memories as we experience interesting events and it is vital for health and well-being that we continue to do so into old age to guard against only living in the past and no longer living *for* anything in the present.

Then there is the 'private' self that talks to the conscious mind, leads and judges, ruminates, worries and controls. This is the self that is a function of all the past experiences, joys and sufferings and guides our conscious mind. It seeks to protect us by raising doubts, fears and hopes but it can also prevent us from seeing reality as it truly is. The private self contains all our past traumas and all those little black events that we have put at the back of our minds and would rather not recall.

There is the 'public' self that shares with the rest of the world only that which it thinks it should. This is the image we like to present externally in the (often mistaken) belief that it will somehow beneficially enhance our status, the way people think of us and thus how we may think of ourselves. Where this self is not in sync with our private self, we experience disquiet and disharmony. If the image lacks authenticity, so too will our own self-belief and our own inner harmony will suffer.

The 'remembered' self, unlike the present self, is the memory or story we have chosen to create about past events and tends to be not only different from reality but also heavily biased.

When we experience something, whether positive or negative, we have certain sensations and emotions right there and then.

With the passage of time, however, we remember the occasion with different eyes and feelings. We 'remember' different aspects and begin to alter the picture to suit our needs with a heavy bias.

If we experienced a wonderful holiday but the return journey included delays, returning to a different airport, and so on, we may well recall the holiday as 'a bit of a disaster' giving much heavier bias to the few hours of pain compared to the many days of enjoyment.

Similarly, if we experienced a negative event—for example, we stumbled and fell at the end of a mountain climb but with no real harm done (other than to pride)—our remembered self creates a story of heroism in the face of adversity, which will animate many a future conversation.

If we drive over-aggressively on the motorway and exchange 'niceties' with another driver, we know at the time that we are in the wrong but subsequent recollections and what we may say to others about the incident will tend to cast the blame on the other driver.

The remembered self can also confuse itself into thinking that we participated in events that happened to others but only happened to us in our mind. It is said that, as time passes, we have more and more vivid recollections of events that never happened.

These examples are simple and relatively trivial.

But the remembered self, if uncontrolled or too self-serving, can be much more nefarious, leading to serious issues of self-deception, pride, anger, blame and sadness and these can easily destroy relationships and the inner peace we are so diligently seeking to attain.

If we are to accede to the happiness of harmony, we need to be clear and truthful about our 'selves' and take very careful note of what is happening in our minds with absolute honesty. Only with honesty and truth can we grow to become better people.

The alternative is to keep deceiving ourselves and simply living lies. This makes learning and progress impossible and destroys happiness.

You cannot improve what you have persuaded yourself to believe is perfectly alright or cannot see in the first place.

When we criticize others, feel envious, resentful, angry, overlooked, unloved, alone, we are only hurting ourselves and allowing the emotions from our own imaginings of the motives of others to unbalance our inner harmony.

We are allowing these unchecked emotions to rule our heart and damage our soul through lack of discipline.

A disciplined mind brings happiness.
Buddha

We need, in a disciplined way, to take time to become aware of and identify each emotion that overtakes us. We need then to examine carefully where the emotion has come from, why we feel the way we do, whether it is appropriate or justified and, if not, what learning we can gain and what we should do to manage better the effects of these emotions in the future.

If we decide that the emotion is not justified, did we allow it to be created by our subconscious mind and then grow out of all proportion? If it was unhelpful to us, what was it that triggered it? In what way was it disruptive to us? When we attributed our anger or frustration to the actions of others, were we right to do so or were we simply reflecting our own inadequacies and needs? What can we learn and what can we do differently to promote our inner harmony rather than subconsciously destroy it?

Whenever you are about to find fault with someone, ask yourself the following question: what fault of mine most nearly resembles the one I am about to criticize?
Marcus Aurelius

Acceptance

Once we become more aware of our emotions and what their causes and effects are, we come to realize again the Buddhist and Stoic principle that the only aspects of our life that we can really control are our thoughts and our actions and that there is little point in worrying about, let alone attempt to impact, what we cannot control.

Paradoxically, although we will still care deeply about many things, unless we develop, at the same time, a sense of indifference about what we cannot influence or control, we will not be able to focus on what we *can* affect positively, and we will thus be unable to achieve inner peace or harmony.

We have to learn to accept this and to realize that attempting to control what is outside our sphere of influence is a waste of energy and effort and ultimately self-defeating. It is damaging to ourselves and to our external world.

We cannot control the impressions
others form about us, and the effort to do
so only debases our character.
Sharon Lebell

*Remove the judgment, and you have
removed the thought 'I am hurt':
remove the thought 'I am hurt',
and the hurt itself is removed.*
Marcus Aurelius

*There is only one way to happiness and
that is to cease worrying about things
which are beyond the power of our will.*
Epictetus

Acceptance is close to letting go in that it requires us to stop fretting about what others are thinking, being anxious about our image or stressed about what others are or are not saying about us.

As long as we are true to ourselves and living a life whose intention is compassion, peace and love, we can be confident that we are doing the best we can for our own inner peace, the harmony of our soul and our universe.

Allowing external factors outside our control to determine our feelings and our life is a recipe for disharmony and unhappiness. If we feel resentful or angry at another or envious of their achievement, we are allowing them to control our emotions. And they probably don't care anyway! This is the path of fear and doubt, rather than love and peace.

We cannot harbour such emotions and at the same time experience inner harmony.

*If you ever happen to turn your attention
to externals, so as to wish to please anyone,
be assured that you have ruined your scheme
of life. Be contented, then, in everything
with being a philosopher; and, if you wish
to be thought so likewise by anyone, appear
so to yourself, and it will suffice you.*
Epictetus

Acceptance means understanding and accepting ourselves for who we are, with all our faults and failings. Facing up to who we are with honesty, modesty and clear-sightedness is the first step to enable us to learn to be better people by working on those areas that are causing imbalances and disharmony.

*Waste no more time arguing about
what a good man should be. Be one.*
Marcus Aurelius

Learning to live in harmony with oneself means taking the trouble to think about how to be a better person, setting personal goals and practising being that person.

Becoming a good person through understanding, compassion and justice is what the Greek philosophers, Socrates, Plato and Aristotle promulgated and this is also the philosophy of the Stoics. It is also the foundation precept of most religions.

It is only by becoming a better person that we can live in harmony and peace with ourselves. It is only by living in harmony and peace with ourselves that we can live in harmony with the universe and experience the true happiness of harmony.

He who lives in harmony with himself lives in harmony with the universe.

Savouring the moment

Being in the moment, being aware, accepting who we are and the people we are with, without judgment and with reverence and humility, allows us to savour each precious moment with family and friends in a way that transcends the everyday and reaches higher levels of joy.

Consider these scenes:

A family is together, after dinner, sitting on a sofa facing the fire. The grandparents are cuddling the grandchildren who are about to read a children's book before going to bed. The parents are looking on with happiness in their hearts. The children take it in turns to read a page of the book. Occasionally they stumble on a word and are helped through it. Their imagination is stimulated by what they are reading and they are, themselves, fully in the moment too and savouring each second. They continually touch the hand of their grandparents for the warmth of human contact. They occasionally glance at the fire with its dancing flames. They look up at their parents and exchange loving smiles. As they become happily sleepy, a grandparent takes over reading the last page or two. They go to bed and are asleep almost immediately. All have experienced a moment of magic, of pure unadulterated joy and of harmony.

Two colleagues are having a meeting with several others. The subject matter is difficult and significant but fascinating, and both are as curious to learn and understand as they are to contribute to the decision. While they are clearly on a similar wavelength and know it, they recognize and celebrate the fact that, not having the same experiences, they have different skills to bring to the party. They respect each other's point of view completely and support each other unconditionally when they share the same perspective. There are no hidden motives between them. They are not in the business of scoring points, engaging in 'double guessing' or appearing to be cleverer than they are. When they feel they need to change their mind about something because they accept a better argument, they do so openly and without shame or embarrassment. They are looking for the best outcome. They have complete trust. They hardly need to exchange words as a look says it all. They are living a moment of friendship and harmony.

Two friends are enjoying lunch together. They share similar interests and passions and are discussing how to move forward as well as catching up on their respective news. They are so engrossed in their conversation and so fully in the moment that the waiter has to come round twice to collect their order. Eating is secondary to savouring the occasion and enjoying each other's company. They respect, trust and listen actively to each other's thoughts and considerations. They smile frequently. Time has little meaning in such a circumstance. They are experiencing a moment of real happiness.

Being able to savour each moment to the full is one of the greatest joys that human beings can experience, wherever, whenever and with whomsoever that may be. It arises from an awareness of the significance of any moment experienced in a spirit of inner calm and peace.

Controlling ego and self-talk

Savouring each precious moment, learning to accept, enjoy and be enthusiastic about such moments in our life and attaining the happiness of harmony requires an understanding of our ego and its pervasive and damaging nature.

It is simply not possible to attain this harmony if our ego-driven self-talk is allowed to govern our thinking in the way it does, without proper control. Our self-talk, we will recall, is that little voice that is constantly chatting to us based on all our previous experiences and seeking to 'protect' us by keeping us 'the way we are.'

But keeping us the way we are is not always good. In the case of people who have become alcoholics, for example, keeping them the way they are is not helpful. Left unchecked, the self-talk of an alcoholic will say, 'It's ok to have a drink.' 'Only one drink can't do any harm.' 'We'll stop tomorrow.' Without changing our self-talk through re-programming the mind and often, such as in the case of alcoholics and similar addictions, medical treatment, our self-talk will create disharmony and make it impossible to find peace, calm and happiness.

When we think deeply about it, however, most of our self-talk's interventions are ego-driven. Our self-talk is accustomed to encouraging us to say and do things that gain us advantage in some way or another and thus feed our ego. We want, crave even, to be successful, admired, loved and cherished, and to be winners, etc., and our self-talk feeds this need.

Our self-talk helps us to act and say what it thinks will benefit us, based on past experience, and, unless it is overridden by our conscious mind, most of it will be self-serving. For example, if we want to impress so that others think well of us in order to feed our ego, we will speak half-truths, make up stories, even blatantly lie, and act dishonestly or in a way designed to deceive in order to create the 'right' impression. If, for example, we want to make a sale and boost our image as master salespeople, to inflate our pride and ego by giving the impression that we are better than others, we will be tempted to tell only part of the sales story and not paint a totally honest picture. How often do we read about events where people have been deliberately misled at great personal cost?

None of this helps our self-esteem, our self-image or our self-love. And if we cannot love ourselves because of such attitudes, how can we love others? If our ego is constantly encouraging us to win and have our way, we cannot live an honest life or in a state of peace. Only by becoming 'gentle' or ego-less can we achieve a sense of calm and harmony.

Blessed are the gentle,
for they shall inherit the earth.
Matthew 5:5, World English Bible

We need to be very conscious and mindful of what we say and do and constantly, critically and with discipline examine our thoughts and deeds ('the unexamined life is not worth living') to ensure that we are acting and speaking honourably, wisely, compassionately and with love.

Man, know thyself, and you are
going to know the gods.

As we learn to understand and control our ego, live more 'in the moment' and just focus on that, without allowing thoughts of past concerns or future fears to stress our minds or feed our egos, we let go of our tensions, start to enjoy life and begin to really feel and experience the happiness of harmony.

You will enjoy any activity in which you are fully present, any activity that is not just a means to an end. It isn't the action you perform that you really enjoy, but the deep sense of aliveness that flows into it ... This means that when you enjoy doing something, you are really experiencing the joy of Being in its dynamic aspect. That's why anything you enjoy doing connects you with the power behind all creation ... If you feel your life lacks significance or is too stressful or tedious, it is because you haven't brought that dimension into your life yet. Being conscious in what you do has not yet become your main aim.
Eckhart Tolle

Purpose and intention

What, then, is our purpose in life? How important are our intentions?

Intentions are like goals and they will drive our purpose in life. Until we have intentions we simply drift. As we develop our goals and intentions, we exercise choice—'I intend to do this'—and we always have a choice.

We can decide to choose a path of fear and doubt, where we see the world as a place where only the fittest survive. Or we can choose a path of love and compassion, where we see the world as a place where we can help, support and protect our fellow human beings, our world and the universe—now and for future generations.

Our intentions create our reality. If our intentions are founded on the belief that the world is essentially inimical and to be feared, we will reflect this in the choices we make and expressions of anger, guilt, shame, resentment and unhappiness.

If, on the other hand, our intentions are founded on the belief that the world is essentially good, loving and forgiving, we will make decisions and exercise choices that are designed to create harmony and love.

If we believe that we are not responsible for the consequences of our intentions and we behave as though we can remain unaffected by what we do, then the actions we take will reflect this and our world will suffer.

If we believe it is alright to misuse our scientific discoveries for destructive purposes, we should not be surprised if the damage we create reaches horrific dimensions.

If, on the other hand, we believe that scientific discoveries should be used to protect our environment, to heal, to house, to feed, to educate, to nurture, to sustain our world, we are choosing a path of compassion and love.

If we believe it is right to take, and take, and take again everything we can without concern for its effect on other people or the environment, make as much money we can irrespective of the fact this may impoverish many less fortunate than ourselves, cheat and steal at will and take everything we can from the earth while discarding our rubbish indiscriminately and without thought for future generations, we are choosing a path of fear and doubt.

If, on the other hand, we believe that we have an absolute responsibility for protecting our species, our families, our friends and our universe, nurturing and teaching our children and helping to create a world of peace and harmony, we are choosing a path of peace, unity and happiness.

Is it not our duty to enter into a sacred and spiritual pledge with ourselves and with like-minded souls to encourage as many as possible to follow a path of love and compassion, rather than one of fear and doubt? Would this not result in a better world? Or is it all too late? Have we so damaged ourselves and our world that a return to truth, honesty and inner peace is no longer possible?

The Greek philosophers believed that it was always possible, by living a life of wisdom and virtue, to create a better, less selfish, more tolerant, more just and happier society and world. There are still very many good people who are fighting for these values and for justice.

Is it not our role also to promote constructive positive change and to become agents for good ourselves? With effort we can all make a difference to our lives and to the lives of others and bring peace, harmony and concord to our world.

Should this not be our true purpose?

Wisdom, reverence, compassion and love

The happiness of harmony is the achievement of sufficient wisdom, reverence, compassion and love to be committed to the growth, peace and happiness of others and of our world.

It starts with ourselves. If we feel compassion for ourselves, we will feel compassion for others. If we have respect and love for ourselves, we will feel and project respect and love for others. If we can forgive ourselves, we will forgive others. If we learn wisdom, we will be able to impart wisdom to others.

The happiness of harmony is the happiness that comes from being at one and at peace with ourselves and our universe. From there we can help, support and nurture others so that they may find their own inner peace; and empower them to make their contribution in turn.

The answer to the questions 'Who am I?' and 'Why am I here?' should now be much clearer: 'Who am I?' I am a person whose soul, 'a particle of love', is a small fragment of the universe and the 'eternal source' to which I will return … like everyone else. 'Why am I here?' I am here because I wish to be a good person who leaves the world in a better state than it was when I entered it; to have created happiness and joy for those with whom I have had the privilege of sharing my life; to have helped, supported, nurtured, comforted, enjoyed and loved unconditionally, with respect and humility; to have moved closer to the light of universal knowledge that comes from continual reflection, the wisdom and the energy to listen and change, and a state of inner peace and harmony.

To love another person is to see the face of God.

You find peace, not by rearranging the circumstances of your life, but by realizing who you are at the deepest level.
Eckhart Tolle

Are you aware of your impact on others?
On yourself? Are you forgiving? To others?
To yourself? Have you learned from your pain?
Are you compassionate and kind?
Do you realize the power of our wake?
Can you learn from unanticipated uncertainties
in your life? Can you grow from struggle?
Can you embrace your ego?

Can you embrace your own unconditional love?
Do you leave ojas (sweet nectar) instead of
ama (toxic residue) when you exit a room, a job,
a relationship, this life? And what do you do
once you realize you have left ama?
Davidji

The Stairway to Happiness is a message of hope and love.

In a world which seems increasingly stressful, dangerous and unjust, it is easy to feel despondent and a deep sense of despair. After all, how can we seek happiness for ourselves when there is so much suffering in the world? It is almost as if we have no right to be happy when so many are unhappy!

The whole point of *The Stairway to Happiness* is to explain what happiness is, how it is created and achieved and how it can be used for good purposes and, above all, to help others.

We can only start to be truly happy ourselves when we learn to understand that it is through helping others and awakening to what is real and authentic, rather than false and destructive, that we can begin the repairing process.

Creating Happiness is about action, not inaction; about being positive, not negative; about doing rather than complaining; about love and light rather than anger and hatred; about acting with tolerance, respect, cooperation and kindness, rather than selfishness, lack of concern, cynicism and isolation. It is about setting a personal example.

There is a lot of beauty to life and it is the privilege, not to say the duty, of those who can see it to help others see it too, by helping, teaching and healing in whatever way possible.

If awakening to the reality of the cruelty and injustice in our world creates inner turmoil in our soul, then bringing happiness through active service and love for others is the surest way for us to bring peace and harmony.

We may well not be able to save the world. That doesn't mean we shouldn't try. Even if we, individually and collectively, only help one person achieve happiness, it will have been of value to that person and to the universe. That is the core message and aspiration of the book.

Helping one person won't change the whole world. But it could change the whole world for that one person. Think what would happen if we all started helping one person every day, every month, every year!

Smiling is the language of angels
Laughter is the music of happiness
Kindness is the touch of the divine
Love is the essence of the Soul

ABOUT THE AUTHOR

Vernon Sankey was born in France and educated in the UK. He graduated in Modern Languages at Oriel College, Oxford. He went straight from university into industry and spent the next 28 years in various countries, culminating as chief executive of a major international corporation in the UK.

He then became a non-executive director and chairman of several large and small international companies, and is still active in this field today. During this time he has also lectured on leadership and motivation at universities, schools and conferences.

In 1999 he co-founded a coaching and mentoring company where he further developed his knowledge of cognitive psychology to help mentor business executives as well as people in all walks of life.

The Stairway to Happiness is the product of this learning.

Vernon is married with four children and five grandchildren. He lives in Berkshire.

79255670R00126

Made in the USA
Middletown, DE
09 July 2018